CAKE&BAKE BIBLE 2022

DELICIOUS RECIPES TO SURPRISE YOUR GUESTS

GEORGE ANDERSON

Table of Contents

Easter Bonnet Cake 14

Easter Simnel Cake 15

Twelfth Night Cake 17

Microwave Apple Cake 18

Microwave Applesauce Cake 19

Microwave Apple and Walnut Cake 20

Microwave Carrot Cake 21

Microwave Carrot, Pineapple and Nut Cake 22

Microwave Spiced Bran Cakes 24

Microwave Banana and Passion Fruit Cheesecake 25

Microwave Baked Orange Cheesecake 26

Microwave Pineapple Cheesecake 27

Microwave Cherry and Nut Loaf 28

Microwave Chocolate Cake 29

Microwave Chocolate Almond Cake 30

Microwave Double Chocolate Brownies 32

Microwave Chocolate Date Bars 33

Microwave Chocolate Squares 34

Microwave Quick Coffee Cake 35

Microwave Christmas Cake 36

Microwave Crumb Cake 38

Microwave Date Bars 39

Microwave Fig Bread 40

Microwave Flapjacks 41

Microwave Fruit Cake 42

Microwave Fruit and Coconut Squares 43

Microwave Fudge Cake 44

Microwave Gingerbread 45

Microwave Ginger Bars 46

Microwave Golden Cake 47

Microwave Honey and Hazelnut Cake 48

Microwave Chewy Muesli Bars 49

Microwave Nut Cake 50

Microwave Orange Juice Cake 51

Microwave Pavlova 52

Microwave Shortcake 53

Microwave Strawberry Shortcake 54

Microwave Sponge Cake 55

Microwave Sultana Bars 56

Microwave Chocolate Biscuits 57

Microwave Coconut Cookies 58

Microwave Florentines 59

Microwave Hazelnut and Cherry Biscuits 60

Microwave Sultana Biscuits 61

Microwave Banana Bread 62

Microwave Cheese Bread 63

Microwave Walnut Loaf 64

No-bake Amaretti Cake 65

American Crispy Rice Bars 66

Apricot Squares 67

Apricot Swiss Roll Cake 68

Broken Biscuit Cakes 69

No-bake Buttermilk Cake 70

Chestnut Slice 71

Chestnut Sponge Cake 72

Chocolate and Almond Bars 74

Chocolate Crisp Cake 75

Chocolate Crumb Squares 76

Chocolate Fridge Cake... 77

Chocolate and Fruit Cake 78

Chocolate and Ginger Squares 79

Luxury Chocolate and Ginger Squares 80

Honey Chocolate Cookies... 81

Chocolate Layer Cake 82

Nice Chocolate Bars 83

Chocolate Praline Squares.. 84

Coconut Crunchies 85

Crunch Bars 86

Coconut and Raisin Crunchies 87

Coffee Milk Squares 88

No-bake Fruit Cake 89

Fruity Squares 90

Fruit and Fibre Crackles 91

Nougat Layer Cake 92

Milk and Nutmeg Squares 93

Muesli Crunch.. 95

Orange Mousse Squares 96

Peanut Squares 97

Peppermint Caramel Cakes	98
Rice Cookies	99
Rice and Chocolate Toffette	100
Almond Paste	101
Sugar-free Almond Paste	102
Royal Icing	103
Sugar-free Icing	104
Fondant Icing	105
Butter Icing	106
Chocolate Butter Icing	107
White Chocolate Butter Icing	108
Coffee Butter Icing	109
Lemon Butter Icing	110
Orange Butter Icing	111
Cream Cheese Icing	112
Rye Bread with Wheatgerm	113
Sally Lunn	114
Samos Bread	115
Sesame Baps	116
Sourdough Starter	117
Soda Bread	118
Sourdough Bread	119
Sourdough Buns	120
Vienna Loaf	121
Wholemeal Bread	122
Wholemeal Honey Bread	123
Quick Wholemeal Rolls	124

Wholemeal Bread with Walnuts	125
Almond Plait	126
Brioches	128
Plaited Brioche	129
Apple Brioches	130
Tofu and Nut Brioches	132
Chelsea Buns	134
Coffee Buns	136
Crème Fraîche Bread	137
Croissants	138
Wholemeal Sultana Croissants	140
Forest Rounds	142
Nutty Twist	143
Orange Buns	145
Pain Chocolat	147
Pandolce	149
Panettone	151
Apple and Date Loaf	152
Apple and Sultana Bread	153
Apple and Cinnamon Surprises	154
Apricot Tea Bread	156
Apricot and Orange Loaf	157
Apricot and Walnut Loaf	158
Autumn Crown	159
Banana Loaf	161
Wholemeal Banana Bread	162
Banana and Nut Bread	163

Bara Brith	164
Bath Buns	165
Cherry and Honey Loaf	166
Cinnamon and Nutmeg Rolls	167
Cranberry Bread	169
Date and Butter Loaf	170
Date and Banana Bread	172
Date and Orange Loaf	173
Date and Nut Bread	174
Date Tea Bread	175
Date and Walnut Loaf	176
Fig Loaf	177
Fig and Marsala Bread	178
Honey and Fig Rolls	179
Hot Cross Buns	181
Lincolnshire Plum Bread	183
London Buns	184
Irish Country Loaf	186
Malt Loaf	187
Bran Malt Loaf	188
Wholemeal Malt Loaf	189
Freda's Nut Loaf	190
Brazil Nut and Date Loaf	192
Panastan Fruit Bread	194
Pumpkin Loaf	196
Raisin Bread	197
Raisin Soak	198

Rhubarb and Date Bread	199
Rice Bread	200
Rice and Nut Tea Bread	201
Curly Sugar Rolls	203
Selkirk Bannock	205
Sultana and Carob Bread	206
Sultana and Orange Loaf	207
Sultana and Sherry Bread	209
Cottage Tea Bread	210
Tea Cakes	212
Potato Scones	213
Raisin Scones	214
Treacle Scones	215
Treacle and Ginger Scones	216
Sultana Scones	217
Wholemeal Treacle Scones	218
Yoghurt Scones	219
Cheese Scones	220
Wholemeal Herb Scones	221
Salami and Cheese Scones	222
Wholemeal Scones	223
Barbadian Conkies	224
Deep-fried Christmas Biscuits	225
Cornmeal Cakes	226
Crumpets	227
Doughnuts	228
Potato Doughnuts	229

Naan Bread	230
Oat Bannocks	231
Pikelets	232
Easy Drop Scones	233
Maple Drop Scones	234
Griddle Scones	235
Cheesy Griddle Scones	236
Special Scotch Pancakes	237
Fruit Scotch Pancakes	238
Orange Scotch Pancakes	239
Singing Hinny	240
Welsh Cakes	241
Welsh Pancakes	242
Mexican Spiced Corn Bread	243
Swedish Flat Bread	244
Steamed Rye and Sweetcorn Bread	245
Steamed Sweetcorn Bread	246
Wholemeal Chapatis	247
Wholemeal Puris	248
Almond Biscuits	249
Almond Curls	250
Almond Rings	251
Mediterranean Almond Cracks	252
Almond and Chocolate Cookies	253
Amish Fruit and Nut Biscuits	254
Anise Biscuits	255
Banana, Oat and Orange Juice Cookies	256

Basic Biscuits	257
Crunchy Bran Biscuits	258
Sesame Bran Biscuits	259
Brandy Biscuits with Caraway	260
Brandy Snaps	261
Butter Biscuits	262
Butterscotch Biscuits	263
Caramel Biscuits	264
Carrot and Walnut Cookies	265
Orange-iced Carrot and Walnut Biscuits	266
Cherry Biscuits	268
Cherry and Almond Rings	269
Chocolate Butter Biscuits	270
Chocolate and Cherry Rolls	271
Chocolate Chip Biscuits	272
Chocolate and Banana Chip Cookies	273
Chocolate and Nut Bites	274
American Chocolate Chip Cookies	275
Chocolate Creams	276
Chocolate Chip and Hazelnut Cookies	277
Chocolate and Nutmeg Biscuits	278
Chocolate-topped Biscuits	279
Coffee and Chocolate Sandwich Biscuits	280
Christmas Biscuits	282
Coconut Biscuits	283
Corn Biscuits with Fruit Cream	284
Cornish Biscuits	285

Wholemeal Currant Biscuits	286
Date Sandwich Biscuits	287
Digestive Biscuits (Graham Crackers)	288
Easter Biscuits	289
Florentines	290
Chocolate Florentines	291
Luxury Chocolate Florentines	292
Fudge Nut Biscuits	293
German Iced Biscuits	294
Gingersnaps	295
Ginger Biscuits	296
Gingerbread Men	297
Wholemeal Ginger Biscuits	298
Ginger and Rice Biscuits	299
Golden Biscuits	300
Hazelnut Biscuits	301
Crunchy Hazelnut Biscuits	302
Hazelnut and Almond Biscuits	303
Honey Cookies	304
Honey Ratafias	305
Honey and Buttermilk Biscuits	306
Lemon Butter Biscuits	307
Lemon Cookies	308
Melting Moments	309

Easter Bonnet Cake

Makes one 20 cm/8 in cake

75 g/3 oz/1/3 cup muscovado sugar

3 eggs

75 g/3 oz/¾ cup self-raising (self-rising) flour

15 ml/1 tbsp cocoa (unsweetened chocolate) powder

15 ml/1 tbsp warm water

For the filling:

50 g/2 oz/¼ cup butter or margarine, softened

75 g/3 oz/½ cup icing (confectioners') sugar, sifted

For the topping:

100 g/4 oz/1 cup plain (semi-sweet) chocolate

25 g/1 oz/2 tbsp butter or margarine

Ribbon or sugar flowers (optional)

Beat together the sugar and eggs in a heatproof bowl set over a pan of gently simmering water. Continue to beat until the mixture is thick and creamy. Leave to stand for a few minutes, then remove from the heat and beat again until the mixture leaves a trail when the whisk is removed. Fold in the flour and cocoa, then stir in the water. Spoon the mixture into a greased and lined 20 cm/8 in cake tin (pan) and a greased and lined 15 cm/ 6 in cake tin. Bake in a preheated oven at 200°C/400°F/gas mark 6 for 15–20 minutes until well risen and firm to the touch. Leave to cool on a wire rack.

To make the filling, cream together the margarine and icing sugar. Use to sandwich the smaller cake on top of the larger one.

To make the topping, melt the chocolate and butter or margarine in a heatproof bowl set over a pan of gently simmering water. Spoon the topping over the cake and spread with a knife dipped in hot water so that it is completely covered. Decorate round the brim with a ribbon or sugar flowers.

Easter Simnel Cake

Makes one 20 cm/8 in cake

225 g/8 oz/1 cup butter or margarine, softened

225 g/8 oz/1 cup soft brown sugar

Grated rind of 1 lemon

4 eggs, beaten

225 g/8 oz/2 cups plain (all-purpose) flour

5 ml/1 tsp baking powder

2.5 ml/½ tsp grated nutmeg

50 g/2 oz/½ cup cornflour (cornstarch)

100 g/4 oz/2/3 cup sultanas (golden raisins)

100 g/4 oz/2/3 cup raisins

75 g/3 oz/½ cup currants

100 g/4 oz/½ cup glacé (candied) cherries, chopped

25 g/1 oz/¼ cup ground almonds

450 g/1 lb Almond Paste

30 ml/2 tbsp apricot jam (conserve)

1 egg white, beaten

Cream together the butter or mar- garine, sugar and lemon rind until pale and fluffy. Gradually beat in the eggs, then fold in the flour, baking powder, nutmeg and cornflour. Stir in the fruit and almonds. Spoon half the mixture into a greased and lined 20 cm/8 in deep cake tin (pan). Roll out half the almond paste to a circle the size of the cake and place on top of the mixture. Fill with the remaining mixture and bake in a pre-heated oven at 160°C/325°F/gas mark 3 for 2–2½ hours until golden brown. Leave to cool in the tin. When cool, turn out and wrap in greaseproof (waxed) paper. Store in an airtight container for up to three weeks if possible to mature.

To finish the cake, brush the top with the jam. Roll out three-quarters of the remaining almond paste to a 20 cm/8 in circle, neaten the edges and place on top of the cake. Roll the remaining almond paste into 11 balls (to represent the disciples without Judas). Brush the top of the cake with beaten egg white and arrange the balls around the edge of the cake, then brush them with egg white. Place under a hot grill (broiler) for a minute or so to brown it slightly.

Twelfth Night Cake

Makes one 20 cm/8 in cake

225 g/8 oz/1 cup butter or margarine, softened

225 g/8 oz/1 cup soft brown sugar

4 eggs, beaten

225 g/8 oz/2 cups plain (all-purpose) flour

5 ml/1 tsp ground mixed (apple-pie) spice

175 g/6 oz/1 cup sultanas (golden raisins)

100 g/4 oz/2/3 cup raisins

75 g/3 oz/½ cup currants

50 g/2 oz/¼ cup glacé (candied) cherries

50 g/2 oz/1/3 cup chopped mixed (candied) peel

30 ml/2 tbsp milk

12 candles to decorate

Cream together the butter or mar- garine and sugar until pale and fluffy. Gradually beat in the eggs, then fold in the flour, mixed spice, fruit and peel and mix until well blended, adding a little milk if necessary to achieve a soft mixture. Spoon into a greased and lined 20 cm/8 in cake tin (pan) and bake in a preheated oven at 180°C/350°F/gas mark 4 for 2 hours until a skewer inserted in the centre comes out clean. Leave

Microwave Apple Cake

Makes one 23 cm/9 in square

100 g/4 oz/½ cup butter or margarine, softened

100 g/4 oz/½ cup soft brown sugar

30 ml/2 tbsp golden (light corn) syrup

2 eggs, lightly beaten

225 g/8 oz/2 cups self-raising (self-rising) flour

10 ml/2 tsp ground mixed (apple-pie) spice

120 ml/4 fl oz/½ cup milk

2 cooking (tart) apples, peeled, cored and thinly sliced

15 ml/1 tbsp caster (superfine) sugar

5 ml/1 tsp ground cinnamon

Cream together the butter or margarine, brown sugar and syrup until pale and fluffy. Gradually beat in the eggs. Fold in the flour and mixed spice, then stir in the milk until you have a soft consistency. Stir in the apples. Spoon into a greased and base-lined 23 cm/9 in microwave ring mould (tube pan) and microwave on Medium for 12 minutes until firm. Allow to stand for 5 minutes, then turn out upside-down and sprinkle with the caster sugar and cinnamon.

Microwave Applesauce Cake

Makes one 20 cm/8 in cake

100 g/4 oz/½ cup butter or margarine, softened

175 g/6 oz/¾ cup soft brown sugar

1 egg, lightly beaten

175 g/6 oz/1½ cups plain (all-purpose) flour

2.5 ml/½ tsp baking powder

A pinch of salt

2.5 ml/½ tsp ground allspice

1.5 ml/¼ tsp grated nutmeg

1.5 ml/¼ tsp ground cloves

300 ml/½ pt/1¼ cups unsweetened apple purée (sauce)

75 g/3 oz/½ cup raisins

Icing (confectioner's) sugar for dusting

Cream together the butter or mar-garine and brown sugar until light and fluffy. Gradually beat in the egg, then fold in the flour, baking powder, salt and spices alternately with the apple purée and raisins. Spoon into a greased and floured 20 cm/8 in square microwave dish and microwave on High for 12 minutes. Leave to cool in the dish, then cut into squares and dust with icing sugar.

Microwave Apple and Walnut Cake

Makes one 20 cm/8 in cake

175 g/6 oz/¾ cup butter or margarine, softened

100 g/4 oz/½ cup caster (superfine) sugar

3 eggs, lightly beaten

30 ml/2 tbsp golden (light corn) syrup

Grated rind and juice of 1 lemon

175 g/6 oz/1½ cups self-raising (self-rising) flour

50 g/2 oz/½ cup walnuts, chopped

1 eating (dessert) apple, peeled, cored and chopped

100 g/4 oz/2/3 cup icing (confectioner's) sugar

30 ml/2 tbsp lemon juice

15 ml/1 tbsp water

Walnut halves to decorate

Cream together the butter or mar-garine and caster sugar until light and fluffy. Gradually add the eggs, then the syrup, lemon rind and juice. Fold in the flour, chopped nuts and apple. Spoon into a greased 20 cm/8 in round microwave dish and microwave on High for 4 minutes. Remove from the oven and cover with foil. Leave to cool. Mix the icing sugar with the lemon juice and enough of the water to form a smooth icing (frosting). Spread over the cake and decorate with walnut halves.

Microwave Carrot Cake

Makes one 18 cm/7 in cake

100 g/4 oz/½ cup butter or margarine, softened

100 g/4 oz/½ cup soft brown sugar

2 eggs, beaten

Grated rind and juice of 1 orange

2.5 ml/½ tsp ground cinnamon

A pinch of grated nutmeg

100 g/4 oz carrots, grated

100 g/4 oz/1 cup self-raising (self-rising) flour

25 g/1 oz/¼ cup ground almonds

25 g/1 oz/2 tbsp caster (superfine) sugar

For the topping:

100 g/4 oz/½ cup cream cheese

50 g/2 oz/1/3 cup icing (confectioners') sugar, sifted

30 ml/2 tbsp lemon juice

Cream together the butter and sugar until light and fluffy. Gradually beat in the eggs, then stir in the orange juice and rind, the spices and carrots. Fold in the flour, almonds and sugar. Spoon into a greased and lined 18 cm/7 in cake dish and cover with clingfilm (plastic wrap). Microwave on High for 8 minutes until a skewer inserted in the centre comes out clean. Remove the clingfilm and leave to stand for 8 minutes before turning out on to a wire rack to finish cooling. Beat the topping ingredients together, then spread over the cooled cake.

Microwave Carrot, Pineapple and Nut Cake

Makes one 20 cm/8 in cake

225 g/8 oz/1 cup caster (superfine) sugar

2 eggs

120 ml/4 fl oz/½ cup oil

1.5 ml/¼ tsp salt

5 ml/1 tsp bicarbonate of soda (baking soda)

100 g/4 oz/1 cup self-raising (self-rising) flour

5 ml/1 tsp ground cinnamon

175 g/6 oz carrots, grated

75 g/3 oz/¾ cup walnuts, chopped

225 g/8 oz crushed pineapple with its juice

For the icing (frosting):

15 g/½ oz/1 tbsp butter or margarine

50 g/2 oz/¼ cup cream cheese

10 ml/2 tsp lemon juice

Icing (confectioners') sugar, sifted

Line a large ring mould (tube pan) with baking parchment. Cream together the sugar, eggs and oil. Gently stir in the dry ingredients until well combined. Stir in the remaining cake ingredients. Pour the mixture into the prepared mould, stand it on a rack or upturned plate and microwave on High for 13 minutes or until just set. Leave to stand for 5 minutes, then turn out on to a rack to cool.

Meanwhile, make the icing. Put the butter or margarine, cream cheese and lemon juice in a bowl and microwave on High for 30–40 seconds. Gradually beat in enough icing sugar to make a thick consistency and beat until fluffy. When the cake is cold, spread over the icing.

Microwave Spiced Bran Cakes

Makes 15

75 g/3 oz/¾ cup All Bran cereal

250 ml/8 fl oz/1 cup milk

175 g/6 oz/1½ cups plain (all-purpose) flour

75 g/3 oz/1/3 cup caster (superfine) sugar

10 ml/2 tsp baking powder

10 ml/2 tsp ground mixed (apple-pie) spice

A pinch of salt

60 ml/4 tbsp golden (light corn) syrup

45 ml/3 tbsp oil

1 egg, lightly beaten

75 g/3 oz/½ cup raisins

15 ml/1 tbsp grated orange rind

Soak the cereal in the milk for 10 minutes. Mix together the flour, sugar, baking powder, mixed spice and salt, then mix into the cereal. Stir in the syrup, oil, egg, raisins and orange rind. Spoon into paper cases (cupcake papers) and microwave five cakes at a time on High for 4 minutes. Repeat for the remaining cakes.

Microwave Banana and Passion Fruit Cheesecake

Makes one 23 cm/9 in cake

100 g/4 oz/½ cup butter or margarine, melted

175 g/6 oz/1½ cups ginger biscuit (cookie) crumbs

250 g/9 oz/generous 1 cup cream cheese

175 ml/6 fl oz/¾ cup soured (dairy sour) cream

2 eggs, lightly beaten

100 g/4 oz/½ cup caster (superfine) sugar

Grated rind and juice of 1 lemon

150 ml/¼ pt/2/3 cup whipping cream

1 banana, sliced

1 passion fruit, chopped

Mix together the butter or margarine and biscuit crumbs and press into the base and sides of a 23 cm/9 in microwave flan dish. Microwave on High for 1 minute. Leave to cool.

Beat together the cream cheese and soured cream until smooth, then beat in the egg, sugar and lemon juice and rind. Spoon into the base and spread evenly. Cook on Medium for 8 minutes. Leave to cool.

Whip the cream until stiff, then spread over the case. Top with banana slices and spoon the passion fruit flesh over the top.

Microwave Baked Orange Cheesecake

Makes one 20 cm/8 in cake

50 g/2 oz/¼ cup butter or margarine

12 digestive biscuits (Graham crackers), crushed

100 g/4 oz/½ cup caster (superfine) sugar

225 g/8 oz/1 cup cream cheese

2 eggs

30 ml/2 tbsp concentrated orange juice

15 ml/1 tbsp lemon juice

150 ml/¼ pt/2/3 cup soured (dairy sour) cream

A pinch of salt

1 orange

30 ml/2 tbsp apricot jam (conserve)

150 ml/¼ pt/2/3 cup double (heavy) cream

Melt the butter or margarine in a 20 cm/8 in microwave flan dish on High for 1 minute. Stir in the biscuit crumbs and 25 g/1 oz/2 tbsp of the sugar and press over the base and sides of the dish. Cream the cheese with the remaining sugar and the eggs, then stir in the orange and lemon juices, soured cream and salt. Spoon into the case (shell) and microwave on High for 2 minutes. Leave to stand for 2 minutes, then microwave on High for a further 2 minutes. Leave to stand for 1 minute, then microwave on High for 1 minute. Leave to cool.

Peel the orange and remove the segments from the membrane, using a sharp knife. Melt the jam and brush over the top of the cheesecake. Whip the cream and pipe round the edge of the cheesecake, then decorate with the orange segments.

Microwave Pineapple Cheesecake

Makes one 23 cm/9 in cake

100 g/4 oz/½ cup butter or margarine, melted

175 g/6 oz/1½ cups digestive biscuit (Graham cracker) crumbs

250 g/9 oz/generous 1 cup cream cheese

2 eggs, lightly beaten

5 ml/1 tsp grated lemon rind

30 ml/2 tbsp lemon juice

75 g/3 oz/1/3 cup caster (superfine) sugar

400 g/14 oz/1 large can pineapple, drained and crushed

150 ml/¼ pt/2/3 cup double (heavy) cream

Mix together the butter or margarine and biscuit crumbs and press into the base and sides of a 23 cm/9 in microwave flan dish. Microwave on High for 1 minute. Leave to cool.

> **Beat together the cream cheese, eggs, lemon rind and juice and sugar until smooth. Stir in the pineapple and spoon into the base. Microwave on Medium for 6 minutes until firm. Leave to cool.**

Whip the cream until stiff, then pile on top of the cheesecake.

Microwave Cherry and Nut Loaf

Makes one 900 g/2 lb loaf

175 g/6 oz/¾ cup butter or margarine, softened

175 g/6 oz/¾ cup soft brown sugar

3 eggs, beaten

225 g/8 oz/2 cups plain (all-purpose) flour

10 ml/2 tsp baking powder

A pinch of salt

45 ml/3 tbsp milk

75 g/3 oz/1/3 cup glacé (candied) cherries

75 g/3 oz/¾ cup chopped mixed nuts

25 g/1 oz/3 tbsp icing (confectioners') sugar, sifted

Cream together the butter or mar-garine and brown sugar until light and fluffy. Gradually beat in the eggs, then fold in the flour, baking powder and salt. Stir in enough of the milk to make a soft consistency, then stir in the cherries and nuts. Spoon into a greased and lined 900 g/2 lb microwave loaf dish and sprinkle with the sugar. Microwave on High for 7 minutes. Leave to stand for 5 minutes, then turn out on to a wire rack to finish cooling.

Microwave Chocolate Cake

Makes one 18 cm/7 in cake

225 g/8 oz/1 cup butter or margarine, softened

175 g/6 oz/¾ cup caster (superfine) sugar

150 g/5 oz/1¼ cups self-raising (self-rising) flour

50 g/2 oz/¼ cup cocoa (unsweetened chocolate) powder

5 ml/1 tsp baking powder

3 eggs, beaten

45 ml/3 tbsp milk

Mix together all the ingredients and spoon into a greased and lined 18 cm/7 in microwave dish. Microwave on High for 9 minutes until just firm to the touch. Leave to cool in the dish for 5 minutes, then turn out on to a wire rack to finish cooling.

Microwave Chocolate Almond Cake

Makes one 20 cm/8 in cake

For the cake:

100 g/4 oz/½ cup butter or margarine, softened

100 g/4 oz/½ cup caster (superfine) sugar

2 eggs, lightly beaten

100 g/4 oz/1 cup self-raising (self-rising) flour

50 g/2 oz/½ cup cocoa (unsweetened chocolate) powder

50 g/2 oz/½ cup ground almonds

150 ml/¼ pt/2/3 cup milk

60 ml/4 tbsp golden (light corn) syrup

For the icing (frosting):

100 g/4 oz/1 cup plain (semi-sweet) chocolate

25 g/1 oz/2 tbsp butter or margarine

8 whole almonds

To make the cake, cream together the butter or mar-garine and sugar until light and fluffy. Gradually beat in the eggs, then fold in the flour and cocoa, followed by the ground almonds. Stir in the milk and syrup and beat until light and soft. Spoon into a 20 cm/8 in microwave dish lined with clingfilm (plastic wrap) and microwave on High for 4 minutes. Remove from the oven, cover the top with foil and leave to cool slightly, then turn out on to a wire rack to finish cooling.

To make the icing, melt the chocolate and butter or margarine on High for 2 minutes. Beat well. Half-dip the almonds in the chocolate, then leave to set on a piece of greaseproof (waxed) paper. Pour the remaining icing over the cake and spread over the top and down the sides. Decorate with the almonds and leave to set.

Microwave Double Chocolate Brownies

Makes 8

150 g/5 oz/1¼ cups plain (semi-sweet) chocolate, coarsely chopped

75 g/3 oz/1/3 cup butter or margarine

175 g/6 oz/¾ cup soft brown sugar

2 eggs, lightly beaten

150 g/5 oz/1¼ cups plain (all-purpose) flour

2.5 ml/½ tsp baking powder

2.5 ml/½ tsp vanilla essence (extract)

30 ml/2 tbsp milk

Melt 50 g/2 oz/½ cup of the chocolate with the butter or margarine on High for 2 minutes. Beat in the sugar and eggs, then stir in the flour, baking powder, vanilla essence and milk until smooth. Spoon into a greased 20 cm/8 in square microwave dish and microwave on High for 7 minutes. Leave to cool in the dish for 10 minutes. Melt the remaining chocolate on High for 1 minute, then spread over the top of the cake and leave to cool. Cut into squares.

Microwave Chocolate Date Bars

Makes 8

50 g/2 oz/1/3 cup stoned (pitted) dates, chopped

60 ml/4 tbsp boiling water

65 g/2½ oz/1/3 cup butter or margarine, softened

225 g/8 oz/1 cup caster (superfine) sugar

1 egg

100 g/4 oz/1 cup plain (all-purpose) flour

10 ml/2 tsp cocoa (unsweetened chocolate) powder

2.5 ml/½ tsp baking powder

A pinch of salt

25 g/1 oz/¼ cup chopped mixed nuts

100 g/4 oz/1 cup plain (semi-sweet) chocolate, finely chopped

Mix the dates with the boiling water and leave to stand until cool. Cream together the butter or margarine with half the sugar until light and fluffy. Gradually work in the egg, then alternately fold in the flour, cocoa, baking powder and salt and the date mixture. Spoon into a greased and floured 20 cm/8 in square microwave dish. Mix the remaining sugar with the nuts and chocolate and sprinkle over the top, pressing down lightly. Microwave on High for 8 minutes. Leave to cool in the dish before cutting into squares.

Microwave Chocolate Squares

Makes 16

For the cake:

50 g/2 oz/¼ cup butter or margarine

5 ml/1 tsp caster (superfine) sugar

75 g/3 oz/¾ cup plain (all-purpose) flour

1 egg yolk

15 ml/1 tbsp water

175 g/6 oz/1½ cups plain (semi-sweet) chocolate, grated or finely chopped

For the topping:

50g /2 oz/¼ cup butter or margarine

50 g/2 oz/¼ cup caster (superfine) sugar

1 egg

2.5 ml/½ tsp vanilla essence (extract)

100 g/4 oz/1 cup walnuts, chopped

To make the cake, soften the butter or margarine and work in the sugar, flour, egg yolk and water. Spread the mixture evenly in a 20 cm/8 in square microwave dish and microwave on High for 2 minutes. Sprinkle over the chocolate and microwave on High for 1 minute. Spread evenly over the base and leave until hardened.

To make the topping, microwave the butter or margarine on High for 30 seconds. Stir in the remaining topping ingredients and spread over the chocolate. Microwave on High for 5 minutes. Leave to cool, then cut into squares.

Microwave Quick Coffee Cake

Makes one 19 cm/7 in cake

For the cake:

225 g/8 oz/1 cup butter or margarine, softened

225 g/8 oz/1 cup caster (superfine) sugar

225 g/8 oz/2 cups self-raising (self-rising) flour

5 eggs

45 ml/3 tbsp coffee essence (extract)

For the icing (frosting):

30 ml/2 tbsp coffee essence (extract)

175 g/6 oz/¾ cup butter or margarine

Icing (confectioners') sugar, sifted

Walnut halves to decorate

Mix together all the cake ingredients until well blended. Divided between two 19 cm/7 in microwave cake contain-ers and cook each one on high for 5–6 minutes. Remove from the microwave and leave to cool.

Blend together the icing ingredients, sweetening to taste with icing sugar. When cool, sandwich the cakes together with half the icing and spread the rest on top. Decorate with walnut halves.

Microwave Christmas Cake

Makes one 23 cm/9 in cake

150 g/5 oz/2/3 cup butter or margarine, softened

150 g/5 oz/2/3 cup soft brown sugar

3 eggs

30 ml/2 tbsp black treacle (molasses)

225 g/8 oz/2 cups self-raising (self-rising) flour

10 ml/2 tsp ground mixed (apple-pie) spice

2. 5 ml/½ tsp grated nutmeg

2.5 ml/½ tsp bicarbonate of soda (baking soda)

450 g/1 lb/22/3 cups mixed dried fruit (fruit cake mix)

50 g/2 oz/¼ cup glacé (candied) cherries

50 g/2 oz/1/3 cup chopped mixed peel

50 g/2 oz/½ cup chopped mixed nuts

30 ml/2 tbsp brandy

Additional brandy to mature the cake (optional)

Cream together the butter or margarine and sugar until light and fluffy. Gradually beat in the eggs and treacle, then fold in the flour, spices and bicarbonate of soda. Gently stir in the fruit, mixed peel and nuts, then stir in the brandy. Spoon into a base-lined 23 cm/9 in microwave dish and microwave on Low for 45–60 minutes. Leave to cool in the dish for 15 minutes before turning out on to a wire rack to finish cooling.

When cool, wrap the cake in foil and store in a cool, dark place for 2 weeks. If liked, pierce the top of the cake several times with a thin skewer and sprinkle over some additional brandy, then rewrap and store the cake. You can do this several times to create a richer cake.

Microwave Crumb Cake

Makes one 20 cm/8 in cake

300 g/10 oz/1¼ cups caster (superfine) sugar

225 g/8 oz/2 cups plain (all-purpose) flour

10 ml/2 tsp baking powder

5 ml/1 tsp ground cinnamon

100 g/4 oz/½ cup butter or margarine, softened

2 eggs, lightly beaten

100 ml/3½ fl oz/6½ tbsp milk

Mix together the sugar, flour, baking powder and cinnamon. Work in the butter or margarine, then set aside a quarter of the mixture. Mix together the eggs and milk and beat into the larger portion of cake mix. Spoon the mixture into a greased and floured 20 cm/8 in microwave dish and sprinkle with the reserved crumble mix. Microwave on High for 10 minutes. Leave to cool in the dish.

Microwave Date Bars

Makes 12

150 g/5 oz/1¼ cups self-raising (self-raising) flour

175 g/6 oz/¾ cup caster (superfine) sugar

100 g/4 oz/1 cup desiccated (shredded) coconut

100 g/4 oz/2/3 cups stoned (pitted) dates, chopped

50 g/2 oz/½ cup chopped mixed nuts

100 g/4 oz/½ cup butter or margarine, melted

1 egg, lightly beaten

Icing (confectioners') sugar for dusting

Mix together the dry ingredients. Stir in the butter or margarine and egg and mix to a firm dough. Press into the base of a 20 cm/8 in square microwave dish and microwave on Medium for 8 minutes until just firm. Leave in the dish for 10 minutes, then cut into bars and turn out on to a wire rack to finish cooling.

Microwave Fig Bread

Makes one 675 g/1½ lb loaf

100 g/4 oz/2 cups bran

50 g/2 oz/¼ cup soft brown sugar

45 ml/3 tbsp clear honey

100 g/4 oz/2/3 cup dried figs, chopped

50 g/2 oz/½ cup hazelnuts, chopped

300 ml/½ pt/1¼ cups milk

100 g/4 oz/1 cup wholemeal (wholewheat) flour

10 ml/2 tsp baking powder

A pinch of salt

Mix together all the ingredients to a stiff dough. Shape into a microwave loaf dish and level the surface. Cook on High for 7 minutes. Leave to cool in the dish for 10 minutes, then turn out on to a wire rack to finish cooling.

Microwave Flapjacks

Makes 24

175 g/6 oz/¾ cup butter or margarine, softened

50 g/2 oz/¼ cup caster (superfine) sugar

50 g/2 oz/¼ cup soft brown sugar

90 ml/6 tbsp golden (light corn) syrup

A pinch of salt

275 g/10 oz/2½ cups rolled oats

Mix together the butter or margarine and sugars in a large bowl and cook on High for 1 minute. Add the remaining ingredients and stir well. Spoon the mixture into a greased 18 cm/7 in microwave dish and press down lightly. Cook on High for 5 minutes. Leave to cool slightly, then cut into squares.

Microwave Fruit Cake

Makes one 18 cm/7 in cake

175 g/6 oz/¾ cup butter or margarine, softened

175 g/6 oz/¾ cup caster (superfine) sugar

Grated rind of 1 lemon

3 eggs, beaten

225 g/8 oz/2 cups plain (all-purpose) flour

5 ml/1 tsp ground mixed (apple-pie) spice

225 g/8 oz/11/3 cups raisins

225 g/8 oz/11/3 cups sultanas (golden raisins)

50 g/2 oz/¼ cup glacé (candied) cherries

50 g/2 oz/½ cup chopped mixed nuts

15 ml/1 tbsp golden (light corn) syrup

45 ml/3 tbsp brandy

Cream together the butter or mar-garine and sugar until light and fluffy. Mix in the lemon rind, then gradually beat in the eggs. Fold in the flour and mixed spice, then mix in the remaining ingredients. Spoon into a greased and lined 18 cm/7 in round microwave dish and microwave on Low for 35 minutes until a skewer inserted in the centre comes out clean. Leave to cool in the dish for 10 minutes, then turn out on to a wire rack to finish cooling.

Microwave Fruit and Coconut Squares

Makes 8

50 g/2 oz/¼ cup butter or margarine

9 digestive biscuits (Graham crackers), crushed

50 g/2 oz/½ cup desiccated (shredded) coconut

100 g/4 oz/2/3 cup chopped mixed (candied) peel

50 g/2 oz/1/3 cup stoned (pitted) dates, chopped

15 ml/1 tbsp plain (all-purpose) flour

25 g/1 oz/2 tbsp glacé (candied) cherries, chopped

100 g/4 oz/1 cup walnuts, chopped

150 ml/¼ pt/2/3 cup condensed milk

Melt the butter or margarine in a 20 cm/8 in square microwave dish on High for 40 seconds. Stir in the biscuit crumbs and spread evenly over the base of the dish. Sprinkle with the coconut, then with the mixed peel. Mix the dates with the flour, cherries and nuts and sprinkle over the top, then pour over the milk. Microwave on High for 8 minutes. Leave to cool in the dish, then cut into squares.

Microwave Fudge Cake

Makes one 20 cm/8 in cake

150 g/5 oz/1¼ cups plain (all-purpose) flour

5 ml/1 tsp baking powder

A pinch of bicarbonate of soda (baking soda)

A pinch of salt

300 g/10 oz/1¼ cups caster (superfine) sugar

50 g/2 oz/¼ cup butter or margarine, softened

250 ml/8 fl oz/1 cup milk

A few drops of vanilla essence (extract)

1 egg

100 g/4 oz /1 cup plain (semi-sweet) chocolate, chopped

50g /2 oz/½ cup chopped mixed nuts

Chocolate Butter Icing

Mix together the flour, baking powder, bicarbonate of soda and salt. Stir in the sugar, then beat in the butter or margarine, milk and vanilla essence until smooth. Beat in the egg. Microwave three-quarters of the chocolate on High for 2 minutes until melted, then beat into the cake mixture until creamy. Stir in the nuts. Spoon the mixture into two greased and floured 20 cm/8 in microwave dishes and microwave each one separately for 8 minutes. Remove from the oven, cover with foil and leave to cool for 10 minutes, then turn out on to a wire rack to finish cooling. Sandwich together with half the butter icing (frosting), then spread the remaining icing over the top and decorate with the reserved chocolate.

Microwave Gingerbread

Makes one 20 cm/8 in cake

50 g/2 oz/¼ cup butter or margarine

75 g/3 oz/¼ cup black treacle (molasses)

15 ml/1 tbsp caster (superfine) sugar

100 g/4 oz/1 cup plain (all-purpose) flour

5 ml/1 tsp ground ginger

2.5 ml/½ tsp ground mixed (apple-pie) spice

2.5 ml/½ tsp bicarbonate of soda (baking soda)

1 egg, beaten

Place the butter or margarine in a bowl and microwave on High for 30 seconds. Stir in the treacle and sugar and microwave on High for 1 minute. Stir in the flour, spices and bicarbonate of soda. Beat in the egg. Spoon the mixture into a greased 1.5 litre/2½ pint/6 cup dish and microwave on High for 4 minutes. Cool in the dish for 5 minutes, then turn out on to a wire rack to finish cooling.

Microwave Ginger Bars

Makes 12

For the cake:

150 g/5 oz/2/3 cup butter or margarine, softened

50 g/2 oz/¼ cup caster (superfine) sugar

100 g/4 oz/1 cup plain (all-purpose) flour

2.5 ml/½ tsp baking powder

5 ml/1 tsp ground ginger

For the topping:

15 g/½ oz/1 tbsp butter or margarine

15 ml/1 tbsp golden (light corn) syrup

A few drops of vanilla essence (extract)

5 ml/1 tsp ground ginger

50 g/2 oz/1/3 cup icing (confectioners') sugar

To make the cake, cream together the butter or mar-garine and sugar until light and fluffy. Stir in the flour, baking powder and ginger and mix to a smooth dough. Press into a 20 cm/8 in square microwave dish and microwave on Medium for 6 minutes until just firm.

To make the topping, melt the butter or margarine and syrup. Stir in the vanilla essence, ginger and icing sugar and whisk until thick. Spread evenly over the warm cake. Leave to cool in the dish, then cut into bars or squares.

Microwave Golden Cake

Makes one 20 cm/8 in cake

For the cake:

100 g/4 oz/½ cup butter or margarine, softened

100 g/4 oz/½ cup caster (superfine) sugar

2 eggs, lightly beaten

A few drops of vanilla essence (extract)

225 g/8 oz/2 cups plain (all-purpose) flour

10 ml/2 tsp baking powder

A pinch of salt

60 ml/4 tbsp milk

For the icing (frosting):

50 g/2 oz/¼ cup butter or margarine, softened

100 g/4 oz/2/3 cup icing (confectioner's) sugar

A few drops of vanilla essence (extract) (optional)

To make the cake, cream together the butter or margarine and sugar until light and fluffy. Gradually beat in the eggs, then fold in the flour, baking powder and salt. Stir in enough of the milk to give a soft, dropping consistency. Spoon into two greased and floured 20 cm/8 in microwave dishes and cook each cake separately on High for 6 minutes. Remove from the oven, cover with foil and leave to cool for 5 minutes, then turn out on to a wire rack to finish cooling.

To make the icing, beat the butter or margarine until soft, then beat in the icing sugar and vanilla essence, if liked. Sandwich the cakes together with half the icing, then spread the remainder over the top.

Microwave Honey and Hazelnut Cake

Makes one 18 cm/7 in cake

150 g/5 oz/2/3 cup butter or margarine, softened

100 g/4 oz/½ cup soft brown sugar

45 ml/3 tbsp clear honey

3 eggs, beaten

225 g/8 oz/2 cups self-raising (self-rising) flour

100 g/4 oz/1 cup ground hazelnuts

45 ml/3 tbsp milk

Butter Icing

Cream together the butter or margarine, sugar and honey until light and fluffy. Gradually beat in the eggs, then fold in the flour and hazelnuts and enough of the milk to give a soft consistency. Spoon into an 18 cm/7 in microwave dish and cook on Medium for 7 minutes. Leave to cool in the dish for 5 minutes, then turn out on to a wire rack to finish cooling. Cut the cake in half horizontally, then sandwich together with butter icing (frosting).

Microwave Chewy Muesli Bars

Makes about 10

100 g/4 oz/½ cup butter or margarine

175 g/6 oz/½ cup clear honey

50 g/2 oz/1/3 cup ready-to-eat dried apricots, chopped

50 g/2 oz/1/3 cup stoned (pitted) dates, chopped

75 g/3 oz/¾ cup chopped mixed nuts

100 g/4 oz/1 cup rolled oats

100 g/4 oz/½ cup soft brown sugar

1 egg, beaten

25 g/1 oz/2 tbsp self-raising (self-rising) flour

Place the butter or margarine and honey in a bowl and cook on High for 2 minutes. Mix in all the remaining ingredients. Spoon into a 20 cm/8 in microwave baking tray and microwave on High for 8 minutes. Leave to cool slightly, then cut into squares or slices.

Microwave Nut Cake

Makes one 20 cm/8 in cake

150 g/5 oz/1¼ cups plain (all-purpose) flour

A pinch of salt

5 ml/1 tsp ground cinnamon

75 g/3 oz/1/3 cup soft brown sugar

75 g/3 oz/1/3 cup caster (superfine) sugar

75 ml/5 tbsp oil

25 g/1 oz/¼ cup walnuts, chopped

5 ml/1 tsp baking powder

2.5 ml/½ tsp bicarbonate of soda (baking soda)

1 egg

150 ml/¼ pt/2/3 cup soured milk

Mix together the flour, salt and half the cinnamon. Stir in the sugars, then beat in the oil until well mixed. Remove 90 ml/6 tbsp of the mixture and stir it into the nuts and remaining cinnamon. Add the baking powder, bicarbonate of soda, egg and milk to the bulk of the mixture and beat until smooth. Spoon the main mixture into a greased and floured 20 cm/8 in microwave dish and sprinkle the nut mixture over the top. Microwave on High for 8 minutes. Leave to cool in the dish for 10 minutes and serve warm.

Microwave Orange Juice Cake

Makes one 20 cm/8 in cake

250 g/9 oz/2¼ cups plain (all-purpose) flour

225 g/8 oz/1 cup granulated sugar

15 ml/1 tbsp baking powder

2.5 ml/½ tsp salt

60 ml/4 tbsp oil

250 ml/8 fl oz/2 cups orange juice

2 eggs, separated

100 g/4 oz/½ cup caster (superfine) sugar

Orange Butter Icing

Orange Glacé Icing

Mix together the flour, granulated sugar, baking powder, salt, oil and half the orange juice and beat until well blended. Beat in the egg yolks and remaining orange juice until light and soft. Whisk the egg whites until stiff, then add half the caster sugar and beat until thick and glossy. Fold in the remaining sugar, then fold the egg whites into the cake mixture. Spoon into two greased and floured 20 cm/8 in microwave dishes and microwave each one separately on High for 6–8 minutes. Remove from the oven, cover with foil and leave to cool for 5 minutes, then turn out on to a wire rack to finish cooling. Sandwich the cakes together with orange butter icing (frosting) and spread the orange glacé icing over the top.

Microwave Pavlova

Makes one 23 cm/9 in cake

4 egg whites

225 g/8 oz/1 cup caster (superfine) sugar

2.5 ml/½ tsp vanilla essence (extract)

A few drops of wine vinegar

150 ml/¼ pt/2/3 cup whipping cream

1 kiwi fruit, sliced

100 g/4 oz strawberries, sliced

Beat the egg whites until they form soft peaks. Sprinkle in half the sugar and beat well. Gradually add the rest of the sugar, the vanilla essence and vinegar and beat until dissolved. Spoon the mixture into to a 23 cm/9 in circle on a piece of baking parchment. Microwave on High for 2 minutes. Leave to stand in the microwave with the door open for 10 minutes. Remove from the oven, tear off the backing paper and leave to cool. Whip the cream until stiff and spread over the top of the meringue. Arrange the fruit attractively on top.

Microwave Shortcake

Makes one 20 cm/8 in cake

225 g/8 oz/2 cups plain (all-purpose) flour

15 ml/1 tbsp baking powder

50 g/2 oz/¼ cup caster (superfine) sugar

100 g/4 oz/½ cup butter or margarine

75 ml/5 tbsp single (light) cream

1 egg

Mix together the flour, baking powder and sugar, then rub in the butter or margarine until the mixture resembles breadcrumbs. Mix together the cream and egg, then work into the flour mixture until you have a soft dough. Press into a greased 20 cm/8 in microwave dish and microwave on High for 6 minutes. Leave to stand for 4 minutes, then turn out and finish cooling on a wire rack.

Microwave Strawberry Shortcake

Makes one 20 cm/8 in cake

900 g/2 lb strawberries, thickly sliced

225 g/8 oz/1 cup caster (superfine) sugar

225 g/8 oz/2 cups plain (all-purpose) flour

15 ml/1 tbsp baking powder

175 g/6 oz/¾ cup butter or margarine

75 ml/5 tbsp single (light) cream

1 egg

150 ml/¼ pt/2/3 cup double (heavy) cream, whipped

Mix the strawberries with 175 g/ 6 oz/¾ cup of the sugar, then chill for at least 1 hour.

Mix together the flour, baking powder and remaining sugar, then rub in 100 g/ 4 oz/½ cup of the butter or margarine until the mixture resembles breadcrumbs. Mix together the single cream and egg, then work into the flour mixture until you have a soft dough. Press into a greased 20 cm/8 in microwave dish and microwave on High for 6 minutes. Leave to stand for 4 minutes, then turn out and split through the centre while still warm. Leave to cool.

Spread both cut surfaces with the remaining butter or margarine. Spread one-third of the whipped cream over the base, then cover with three-quarters of the strawberries. Top with a further one-third of the cream, then place the second shortcake on top. Top with the remaining cream and strawberries.

Microwave Sponge Cake

Makes one 18 cm/7 in cake

150 g/5 oz/1¼ cups self-raising (self-rising) flour

100 g/4 oz/½ cup butter or margarine

100 g/4 oz/½ cup caster (superfine) sugar

2 eggs

30 ml/2 tbsp milk

Beat together all the ingredients until smooth. Spoon into a base-lined 18 cm/7 in microwave dish and microwave on Medium for 6 minutes. Leave to cool in the dish for 5 minutes, then turn out on to a wire rack to finish cooling.

Microwave Sultana Bars

Makes 12

175 g/6 oz/¾ cup butter or margarine

100 g/4 oz/½ cup caster (superfine) sugar

15 ml/1 tbsp golden (light corn) syrup

75 g/3 oz/½ cup sultanas (golden raisins)

5 ml/1 tsp grated lemon rind

225 g/8 oz/2 cups self-raising (self-rising) flour

For the icing (frosting):
175 g/6 oz/1 cup icing (confectioners') sugar

30 ml/2 tbsp lemon juice

Microwave the butter or margarine, caster sugar and syrup on Medium for 2 minutes. Stir in the sultanas and lemon rind. Fold in the flour. Spoon into a greased and lined 20 cm/8 in square microwave dish and microwave on Medium for 8 minutes until just firm. Leave to cool slightly.

Place the icing sugar in a bowl and make a well in the centre. Gradually mix in the lemon juice to make a smooth icing. Spread over the cake while still just warm, then leave to cool completely.

Microwave Chocolate Biscuits

Makes 24

225 g/8 oz/1 cup butter or margarine, softened

100 g/4 oz/½ cup dark brown sugar

5 ml/1 tsp vanilla essence (extract)

225 g/8 oz/2 cups self-raising (self-rising) flour

50 g/2 oz/½ cup drinking chocolate powder

Cream together the butter, sugar and vanilla essence until light and fluffy. Gradually mix in the flour and chocolate and mix to a smooth dough. Shape into walnut-sized balls, arrange six at a time on a greased microwave baking (cookie) sheet and flatten slightly with a fork. Microwave each batch on High for 2 minutes, until all the biscuits (cookies) are cooked. Leave to cool on a wire rack.

Microwave Coconut Cookies

Makes 24

50 g/2 oz/¼ cup butter or margarine, softened

75 g/3 oz/1/3 cup caster (superfine) sugar

1 egg, lightly beaten

2.5 ml/½ tsp vanilla essence (extract)

75 g/3 oz/¾ cup plain (all-purpose) flour

25 g/1 oz/¼ cup desiccated (shredded) coconut

A pinch of salt

30 ml/2 tbsp strawberry jam (conserve)

Beat together the butter or margarine and sugar until light and fluffy. Stir in the egg and vanilla essence alternately with the flour, coconut and salt and mix to a smooth dough. Shape into walnut-sized balls and arrange six at a time on a greased microwave baking (cookie) sheet, then press lightly with a fork to flatten slightly. Microwave on High for 3 minutes until just firm. Transfer to a wire rack and place a spoonful of jam on the centre of each cookie. Repeat with the remaining cookies.

Microwave Florentines

Makes 12

50 g/2 oz/¼ cup butter or margarine

50 g/2 oz/¼ cup demerara sugar

15 ml/1 tbsp golden (light corn) syrup

50 g/2 oz/¼ cup glacé (candied) cherries

75 g/3 oz/¾ cup walnuts, chopped

25 g/1 oz/3 tbsp sultanas (golden raisins)

25 g/1 oz/¼ cup flaked (slivered) almonds

30 ml/2 tbsp chopped mixed (candied) peel

25 g/1 oz/¼ cup plain (all-purpose) flour

100 g/4 oz/1 cup plain (semi-sweet) chocolate, broken up (optional)

Microwave the butter or margarine, sugar and syrup on High for 1 minute until melted. Stir in the cherries, walnuts, sultanas and almonds, then mix in the mixed peel and flour. Place teaspoonfuls of the mixture, well apart, on greaseproof (waxed) paper and cook four at a time on High for 1½ minutes each batch. Neaten the edges with a knife, leave to cool on the paper for 3 minutes, then transfer to a wire rack to finish cooling. Repeat with the remaining biscuits. If liked, melt the chocolate in a bowl for 30 seconds and spread over one side of the florentines, then leave to set.

Microwave Hazelnut and Cherry Biscuits

Makes 24

100 g/4 oz/½ cup butter or margarine, softened

100 g/4 oz/½ cup caster (superfine) sugar

1 egg, beaten

175 g/6 oz/1½ cups plain (all-purpose) flour

50 g/2 oz/½ cup ground hazelnuts

100 g/4 oz/½ cup glacé (candied) cherries

Cream together the butter or margarine and sugar until light and fluffy. Gradually beat in the egg, then fold in the flour, hazelnuts and cherries. Place spoonfuls well spaced out on microwave baking (cookie) sheets and microwave eight biscuits (cookies) at a time on High for about 2 minutes until just firm.

Microwave Sultana Biscuits

Makes 24

225 g/8 oz/2 cups plain (all-purpose) flour

5 ml/1 tsp ground mixed (apple-pie) spice

175 g/6 oz/¾ cup butter or margarine, softened

100 g/4 oz/2/3 cup sultanas (golden raisins)

175 g/6 oz/¾ cup demerara sugar

Mix together the flour and mixed spice, then blend in the butter or margarine, sultanas and 100 g/4 oz/½ cup of the sugar to make a soft dough. Roll into two sausage shapes about 18 cm/7 in long and roll in the remaining sugar. Cut into slices and arrange six at a time on a greased microwave baking (cookie) sheet and microwave on High for 2 minutes. Leave to cool on a wire rack and repeat with the remaining biscuits (cookies).

Microwave Banana Bread

Makes one 450 g/1 lb loaf

75 g/3 oz/1/3 cup butter or margarine, softened

175 g/6 oz/¾ cup caster (superfine) sugar

2 eggs, lightly beaten

200 g/7 oz/1¾ cups plain (all-purpose) flour

10 ml/2 tsp baking powder

2.5 ml/½ tsp bicarbonate of soda (baking soda)

A pinch of salt

2 ripe bananas

15 ml/1 tbsp lemon juice

60 ml/4 tbsp milk

50 g/2 oz/½ cup walnuts, chopped

Cream together the butter or margarine and sugar until light and fluffy. Gradually beat in the eggs, then fold in the flour, baking powder, bicarbonate of soda and salt. Mash the bananas with the lemon juice, then fold into the mixture with the milk and walnuts. Spoon into a greased and floured 450 g/1 lb microwave loaf tin (pan) and microwave on High for 12 minutes. Remove from the oven, cover with foil and leave to cool for 10 minutes, then turn out on to a wire rack to finish cooling.

Microwave Cheese Bread

Makes one 450 g/1 lb loaf

50 g/2 oz/¼ cup butter or margarine

250 ml/8 fl oz/1 cup milk

2 eggs, lightly beaten

225 g/8 oz/2 cups plain (all-purpose) flour

10 ml/2 tsp baking powder

10 ml/2 tsp mustard powder

2.5 ml/½ tsp salt

175 g/6 oz/1½ cups Cheddar cheese, grated

Melt the butter or margarine in a small bowl on High for 1 minute. Stir in the milk and eggs. Mix together the flour, baking powder, mustard, salt and 100 g/4 oz/1 cup of the cheese. Stir in the milk mixture until well blended. Spoon into a microwave loaf tin (pan) and microwave on High for 9 minutes. Sprinkle with the remaining cheese, cover with foil and leave to stand for 20 minutes.

Microwave Walnut Loaf

Makes one 450 g/1 lb loaf

225 g/8 oz/2 cups plain (all-purpose) flour

300 g/10 oz/1¼ cups caster (superfine) sugar

5 ml/1 tsp baking powder

A pinch of salt

100 g/4 oz/½ cup butter or margarine, softened

150 ml/¼ pt/2/3 cup milk

2.5 ml/½ tsp vanilla essence (extract)

4 egg whites

50 g/2 oz/½ cup walnuts, chopped

Mix together the flour, sugar, baking powder and salt. Beat in the butter or margarine, then the milk and vanilla essence. Beat in the egg whites until creamy, then fold in the nuts. Spoon into a greased and floured 450 g/1 lb microwave loaf tin (pan) and microwave on High for 12 minutes. Remove from the oven, cover with foil and leave to cool for 10 minutes, then turn out on to a wire rack to finish cooling.

No-bake Amaretti Cake

Makes one 20 cm/8 in cake

100 g/4 oz/½ cup butter or margarine

175 g/6 oz/1½ cups plain (semi-sweet) chocolate

75 g/3 oz Amaretti biscuits (cookies), coarsely crushed

175 g/6 oz/1½ cups walnuts, chopped

50 g/2 oz/½ cup pine nuts

75 g/3 oz/1/3 cup glacé (candied) cherries, chopped

30 ml/2 tbsp Grand Marnier

225 g/8 oz/1 cup Mascarpone cheese

Melt the butter or margarine and chocolate in a heatproof bowl set over a pan of gently simmering water. Remove from the heat and stir in the biscuits, nuts and cherries. Spoon into a sandwich tin (pan) lined with clingfilm (plastic wrap) and press down gently. Chill for 1 hour until set. Turn out on to a serving plate and remove the clingfilm. Beat the Grand Marnier into the Mascarpone and spoon over the base.

American Crispy Rice Bars

Makes about 24 bars

50 g/2 oz/¼ cup butter or margarine

225 g/8 oz white marshmallows

5 ml/1 tsp vanilla essence (extract)

150 g/5 oz/5 cups puffed rice cereal

Melt the butter or margarine in a large pan over a low heat. Add the marshmallows and cook, stirring continuously, until the marshmallows have melted and the mixture is syrupy. Remove from the heat and add the vanilla essence. Stir in the rice cereal until evenly coated. Press into a 23 cm/9 in square tin (pan) and cut into bars. Leave to set.

Apricot Squares

Makes 12

50 g/2 oz/¼ cup butter or margarine

175 g/6 oz/1 small can evaporated milk

15 ml/1 tbsp clear honey

45 ml/3 tbsp apple juice

50 g/2 oz/¼ cup soft brown sugar

50 g/2 oz/1/3 cup sultanas (golden raisins)

225 g/8 oz/11/3 cups ready-to-eat dried apricots, chopped

100 g/4 oz/1 cup desiccated (shredded) coconut

225 g/8 oz/2 cups rolled oats

Melt the butter or margarine with the milk, honey, apple juice and sugar. Stir in the remaining ingredients. Press into a greased 25 cm/12 in baking tin (pan) and chill before cutting into squares.

Apricot Swiss Roll Cake

Makes one 23 cm/9 in cake

400 g/14 oz/1 large can apricot halves, drained and juice reserved

50 g/2 oz/½ cup custard powder

75 g/3 oz/¼ cup apricot jelly (clear conserve)

75 g/3 oz/½ cup ready-to-eat dried apricots, chopped

400 g/14 oz/1 large can condensed milk

225 g/8 oz/1 cup cottage cheese

45 ml/3 tbsp lemon juice

1 Swiss Roll, sliced

Make up the apricot juice with water to make 500 ml/17 fl oz/2¼ cups. Mix the custard powder to a paste with a little of the liquid, then bring the remainder to the boil. Stir in the custard paste and apricot jelly and simmer until thick and shiny, stirring continuously. Mash the canned apricots and add to the mixture with the dried apricots. Leave to cool, stirring occasionally.

Beat together the condensed milk, cottage cheese and lemon juice until well blended, then stir into the jelly mixture. Line a 23 cm/9 in cake tin (pan) with clingfilm (plastic wrap) and arrange the Swiss (jelly) roll slices over the base and sides of the tin. Spoon in the cake mixture and chill until set. Turn out carefully when ready to serve.

Broken Biscuit Cakes

Makes 12

100 g/4 oz/½ cup butter or margarine

30 ml/2 tbsp caster (superfine) sugar

15 ml/1 tbsp golden (light corn) syrup

30 ml/2 tbsp cocoa (unsweetened chocolate) powder

225 g/8 oz/2 cups broken biscuit (cookie) crumbs

50 g/2 oz/1/3 cup sultanas (golden raisins)

Melt the butter or margarine with the sugar and syrup without allowing the mixture to boil. Stir in the cocoa, biscuits and sultanas. Press into a greased 25 cm/10 in baking tin (pan), leave to cool, then chill until firm. Cut into squares.

No-bake Buttermilk Cake

Makes one 23 cm/9 in cake

30 ml/2 tbsp custard powder

100 g/4 oz/½ cup caster (superfine) sugar

450 ml/¾ pt/2 cups milk

175 ml/6 fl oz/¾ cup buttermilk

25 g/1 oz/2 tbsp butter or margarine

400 g/12 oz plain biscuits (cookies), crushed

120 ml/4 fl oz/½ cup whipping cream

Blend the custard powder and sugar to a paste with a little of the milk. Bring the remaining milk to the boil. Stir it into the paste, then return the whole mixture to the pan and stir over a low heat for about 5 minutes until thickened. Stir in the buttermilk and butter or margarine. Spoon layers of crushed biscuits and custard mixture into a 23 cm/9 in cake tin (pan) lined with clingfilm (plastic wrap), or into a glass dish. Press down gently and chill until set. Whip the cream until stiff, then pipe rosettes of cream on the top of the cake. Either serve from the dish, or lift out carefully to serve.

Chestnut Slice

Makes one 900 g/2 lb loaf

225 g/8 oz/2 cups plain (semi-sweet) chocolate

100 g/4 oz/½ cup butter or margarine, softened

100 g/4 oz/½ cup caster (superfine) sugar

450 g/1 lb/1 large can unsweetened chestnut purée

25 g/1 oz/¼ cup rice flour

A few drops of vanilla essence (extract)

150 ml/¼ pt/2/3 cup whipping cream, whipped

Grated chocolate to decorate

Melt the plain chocolate in a heatproof bowl over a pan of gently simmering water. Cream together the butter or margarine and sugar until light and fluffy. Beat in the chestnut purée, chocolate, rice flour and vanilla essence. Turn into a greased and lined 900 g/2 lb loaf tin (pan) and chill until firm. Decorate with whipped cream and grated chocolate before serving.

Chestnut Sponge Cake

Makes one 900 g/2 lb cake

For the cake:

400 g/14 oz/1 large can sweetened chestnut purée

100 g/4 oz/½ cup butter or margarine, softened

1 egg

A few drops of vanilla essence (extract)

30 ml/2 tbsp brandy

24 sponge finger biscuits (cookies)

For the glaze:

30 ml/2 tbsp cocoa (unsweetened chocolate) powder

15 ml/1 tbsp caster (superfine) sugar

30 ml/2 tbsp water

For the butter cream:

100 g/4 oz/½ cup butter or margarine, softened

100 g/4 oz/2/3 cup icing (confectioners') sugar, sifted

15 ml/1 tbsp coffee essence (extract)

To make the cake, blend together the chestnut purée, butter or margarine, egg, vanilla essence and 15 ml/1 tbsp of the brandy and beat until smooth. Grease and line a 900 g/2 lb loaf tin (pan) and line the base and sides with the sponge fingers. Sprinkle the remaining brandy over the biscuits and spoon the chestnut mixture into the centre. Chill until firm.

Lift out of the tin and remove the lining paper. Dissolve the glaze ingredients in a heatproof bowl set over a pan of gently simmering water, stirring until smooth. Leave to cool slightly, then brush most of the glaze over the top of the cake. Cream together the butter cream ingredients until smooth, then pipe into swirls around the edge of the cake. Drizzle with the reserved glaze to finish.

Chocolate and Almond Bars

Makes 12

175 g/6 oz/1½ cups plain (semi-sweet) chocolate, chopped

3 eggs, separated

120 ml/4 fl oz/½ cup milk

10 ml/2 tsp powdered gelatine

120 ml/4 fl oz/½ cup double (heavy) cream

45 ml/3 tbsp caster (superfine) sugar

60 ml/4 tbsp flaked (slivered) almonds, toasted

Melt the chocolate in a heatproof bowl set over a pan of gently simmering water. Remove from the heat and beat in the egg yolks. Boil the milk in a separate pan, then whisk in the gelatine. Stir into the chocolate mixture, then stir in the cream. Beat the egg whites until stiff, then add the sugar and beat again until stiff and glossy. Fold into the mixture. Spoon into a greased and lined 450 g/1 lb loaf tin (pan), sprinkle with the toasted almonds and leave to cool, then chill for at least 3 hours until set. Turn over and cut into thick slices to serve

Chocolate Crisp Cake

Makes one 450 g/1 lb loaf

150 g/5 oz/2/3 cup butter or margarine
30 ml/2 tbsp golden (light corn) syrup

175 g/6 oz/1½ cups digestive biscuit (Graham cracker) crumbs

50 g/2 oz/2 cups puffed rice cereal

25 g/1 oz/3 tbsp sultanas (golden raisins)

25 g/1 oz/2 tbsp glacé (candied) cherries, chopped

225 g/8 oz/2 cups chocolate chips

30 ml/2 tbsp water

175 g/6 oz/1 cup icing (confectioners') sugar, sifted

Melt 100 g/4 oz/½ cup of the butter or margarine with the syrup, then remove from the heat and stir in the biscuit crumbs, cereal, sultanas, cherries and three-quarters of the chocolate chips. Spoon into a greased and lined 450 g/1 lb loaf tin (pan) and smooth the top. Chill until firm. Melt the remaining butter or margarine with the remaining chocolate and the water. Stir in the icing sugar and mix until smooth. Remove the cake from the tin and halve lengthways. Sandwich together with half the chocolate icing (frosting), place on a serving plate, then pour over the remaining icing. Chill before serving.

Chocolate Crumb Squares

Makes about 24

225 g/8 oz digestive biscuits (Graham crackers)

100 g/4 oz/½ cup butter or margarine

25 g/1 oz/2 tbsp caster (superfine) sugar

15 ml/1 tbsp golden (light corn) syrup

45 ml/3 tbsp cocoa (unsweetened chocolate) powder

200 g/7 oz/1¾ cups chocolate cake covering

Place the biscuits in a plastic bag and crush with a rolling pin. Melt the butter or margarine in a pan, then stir in the sugar and syrup. Remove from the heat and stir in the biscuit crumbs and cocoa. Turn into a greased and lined 18 cm/7 in square cake tin and press down evenly. Leave to cool, then chill in the fridge until set.

Melt the chocolate in a heatproof bowl set over a pan of gently simmering water. Spread over the biscuit, marking into lines with a fork while setting. Cut into squares when firm.

Chocolate Fridge Cake

Makes one 450 g/1 lb cake

100 g/4 oz/½ cup soft brown sugar

100 g/4 oz/½ cup butter or margarine

50 g/2 oz/½ cup drinking chocolate powder

25 g/1 oz/¼ cup cocoa (unsweetened chocolate) powder

30 ml/2 tbsp golden (light corn) syrup

150 g/5 oz digestive biscuits (Graham crackers) or rich tea biscuits

50 g/2 oz/¼ cup glacé (candied) cherries or mixed nuts and raisins

100 g/4 oz/1 cup milk chocolate

Place the sugar, butter or margarine, drinking chocolate, cocoa and syrup in a pan and warm gently until the butter has melted, stirring well. Remove from the heat and crumble in the biscuits. Stir in the cherries or nuts and raisins and spoon into a 450 g/1 lb loaf tin (pan). Leave in the fridge to cool.

Melt the chocolate in a heatproof bowl over a pan of gently simmering water. Spread over the top of the cooled cake and slice when set.

Chocolate and Fruit Cake

Makes one 18 cm/7 in cake

100 g/4 oz/½ cup butter or margarine, melted

100 g/4 oz/½ cup soft brown sugar

225 g/8 oz/2 cups digestive biscuit (Graham cracker) crumbs

50 g/2 oz/1/3 cup sultanas (golden raisins)

45 ml/3 tbsp cocoa (unsweetened chocolate) powder

1 egg, beaten

A few drops of vanilla essence (extract)

Mix the butter or margarine and sugar, then stir in the remaining ingredients and beat well. Spoon into a greased 18 cm/7 in sandwich tin (pan) and smooth the surface. Chill until set.

Chocolate and Ginger Squares

Makes 24

100 g/4 oz/½ cup butter or margarine

100 g/4 oz/½ cup soft brown sugar

30 ml/2 tbsp cocoa (unsweetened chocolate) powder

1 egg, lightly beaten

225 g/8 oz/2 cups ginger biscuit (cookie) crumbs

15 ml/1 tbsp chopped crystallised (candied) ginger

Melt the butter or margarine, then stir in the sugar and cocoa until well blended. Mix in the egg, biscuit crumbs and ginger. Press into a Swiss roll tin (jelly roll pan) and chill until firm. Cut into squares.

Luxury Chocolate and Ginger Squares

Makes 24

100 g/4 oz/½ cup butter or margarine

100 g/4 oz/½ cup soft brown sugar

30 ml/2 tbsp cocoa (unsweetened chocolate) powder

1 egg, lightly beaten

225 g/8 oz/2 cups ginger biscuit (cookie) crumbs

15 ml/1 tbsp chopped crystallised (candied) ginger

100 g/4 oz/1 cup plain (semi-sweet) chocolate

Melt the butter or margarine, then stir in the sugar and cocoa until well blended. Mix in the egg, biscuit crumbs and ginger. Press into a Swiss roll tin (jelly roll pan) and chill until firm.

Melt the chocolate in a heatproof bowl set over a pan of gently simmering water. Spread over the cake and leave to set. Cut into squares when the chocolate is almost hard.

Honey Chocolate Cookies

Makes 12

225 g/8 oz/1 cup butter or margarine

30 ml/2 tbsp clear honey

90 ml/6 tbsp carob or cocoa (unsweetened chocolate) powder

225 g/8 oz/2 cups sweet biscuit (cookie) crumbs

Melt the butter or margarine, honey and carob or cocoa powder in a pan until well blended. Mix in the biscuit crumbs. Spoon into a greased 20 cm/8 in square cake tin (pan) and leave to cool, then cut into squares.

Chocolate Layer Cake

Makes one 450 g/1 lb cake

300 ml/½ pt/1¼ cups double (heavy) cream

225 g/8 oz/2 cups plain (semi-sweet) chocolate, broken up

5 ml/1 tsp vanilla essence (extract)

20 plain biscuits (cookies)

Heat the cream in a pan over a low heat until almost boiling. Remove from the heat and add the chocolate, stir, cover and leave for 5 minutes. Stir in the vanilla essence and mix until well blended, then chill until the mixture begins to thicken.

Line a 450g /1 lb loaf tin (pan) with clingfilm (plastic wrap). Spread a layer of chocolate on the bottom, then arrange a few biscuits in a layer on top. Continue layering the chocolate and biscuits until you have used them up. Finish with a layer of chocolate. Cover with clingfilm and chill for at least 3 hours. Turn out the cake and remove the clingfilm.

Nice Chocolate Bars

Makes 12

100 g/4 oz/½ cup butter or margarine

30 ml/2 tbsp golden (light corn) syrup

30 ml/2 tbsp cocoa (unsweetened chocolate) powder

225 g/8 oz/1 packet Nice or plain biscuits (cookies), roughly crushed

100 g/4 oz/1 cup plain (semi-sweet) chocolate, diced

Melt the butter or margarine and syrup, then remove from the heat and stir in the cocoa and crushed biscuits. Spread the mixture in a 23 cm/9 in square cake tin (pan) and level the surface. Melt the chocolate in a heatproof bowl over a pan of gently simmering water and spread over the top. Leave to cool slightly, then cut into bars or squares and chill until set.

Chocolate Praline Squares

Makes 12

100 g/4 oz/½ cup butter or margarine

30 ml/2 tbsp caster (superfine) sugar

15 ml/1 tbsp golden (light corn) syrup

15 ml/1 tbsp drinking chocolate powder

225 g/8 oz digestive biscuits (Graham crackers), crushed

200 g/7 oz/1¾ cups plain (semi-sweet) chocolate

100 g/4 oz/1 cup chopped mixed nuts

Melt the butter or margarine, sugar, syrup and drinking chocolate in a pan. Bring to the boil, then boil for 40 seconds. Remove from the heat and stir in the biscuits and nuts. Press into a greased 28 x 18 cm/11 x 7 in cake tin (pan). Melt the chocolate in a heatproof bowl over a pan of gently simmering water. Spread over the biscuits and leave to cool, then chill for 2 hours before cutting into squares.

Coconut Crunchies

Makes 12

100 g/4 oz/1 cup plain (semi-sweet) chocolate

30 ml/2 tbsp milk

30 ml/2 tbsp golden (light corn) syrup

100 g/4 oz/4 cups puffed rice cereal

50 g/2 oz/½ cup desiccated (shredded) coconut

Melt the chocolate, milk and syrup in a pan. Remove from the heat and stir in the cereal and coconut. Spoon into paper cake cases (cupcake papers) and leave to set.

Crunch Bars

Makes 12

175 g/6 oz/¾ cup butter or margarine

50 g/2 oz/¼ cup soft brown sugar

30 ml/2 tbsp golden (light corn) syrup

45 ml/3 tbsp cocoa (unsweetened chocolate) powder

75 g/3 oz/½ cup raisins or sultanas (golden raisins)

350 g/12 oz/3 cups oat crunch cereal

225 g/8 oz/2 cups plain (semi-sweet) chocolate

Melt the butter or margarine with the sugar, syrup and cocoa. Stir in the raisins or sultanas and the cereal. Press the mixture into a greased 25 cm/12 in baking tin (pan). Melt the chocolate in a heatproof bowl over a pan of gently simmering water. Spread over the bars and leave to cool, then chill before cutting into bars.

Coconut and Raisin Crunchies

Makes 12

100 g/4 oz/1 cup white chocolate

30 ml/2 tbsp milk

30 ml/2 tbsp golden (light corn) syrup

175 g/6 oz/6 cups puffed rice cereal

50 g/2 oz/1/3 cup raisins

Melt the chocolate, milk and syrup in a pan. Remove from the heat and stir in the cereal and raisins. Spoon into paper cake cases (cupcake papers) and leave to set.

Coffee Milk Squares

Makes 20

25 g/1 oz/2 tbsp powdered gelatine

75 ml/5 tbsp cold water

225 g/8 oz/2 cups plain biscuit (cookie) crumbs

50 g/2 oz/¼ cup butter or margarine, melted

400 g/14 oz/1 large can evaporated milk

150 g/5 oz/2/3 cup caster (superfine) sugar

400 ml/14 fl oz/1¾ cups strong black coffee, ice cold

Whipped cream and crystallised (candied) orange slices to decorate

Sprinkle the gelatine over the water in a bowl and leave until spongy. Stand the bowl in a pan of hot water and leave until dissolved. Leave to cool slightly. Stir the biscuit crumbs into the melted butter and press into the base and sides of a greased 30 x 20 cm/12 x 8 in rectangular cake tin (pan). Beat the evaporated milk until thick, then gradually beat in the sugar, followed by the dissolved gelatine and the coffee. Spoon over the base and chill until set. Cut into squares and decorate with piped whipped cream and crystallised (candied) orange slices.

No-bake Fruit Cake

Makes one 23 cm/9 in cake

450 g/1 lb/22/3 cups dried mixed fruit (fruit cake mix)

450 g/1 lb plain biscuits (cookies), crushed

100 g/4 oz/½ cup butter or margarine, melted

100 g/4 oz/½ cup soft brown sugar

400 g/14 oz/1 large can condensed milk

5 ml/1 tsp vanilla essence (extract)

Mix together all the ingredients until well blended. Spoon into a greased 23 cm/9 in cake tin (pan) lined with clingfilm (plastic wrap) and press down. Chill until firm.

Fruity Squares

Makes about 12

100 g/4 oz/½ cup butter or margarine

100 g/4 oz/½ cup soft brown sugar

400 g/14 oz/1 large can condensed milk

5 ml/1 tsp vanilla essence (extract)

250 g/9 oz/1½ cups dried mixed fruit (fruit cake mix)

100 g/4 oz/½ cup glacé (candied) cherries

50 g/2 oz/½ cup chopped mixed nuts

400 g/14 oz plain biscuits (cookies), crushed

Melt the butter or margarine and sugar over a low heat. Stir in the condensed milk and vanilla essence and remove from the heat. Mix in the remaining ingredients. Press into a greased Swiss roll tin (jelly roll pan) and chill for 24 hours until firm. Cut into squares.

Fruit and Fibre Crackles

Makes 12

100 g/4 oz/1 cup plain (semi-sweet) chocolate

50 g/2 oz/¼ cup butter or margarine

15 ml/1 tbsp golden (light corn) syrup

100 g/4 oz/1 cup fruit and fibre breakfast cereal

Melt the chocolate in a heatproof bowl over a pan of gently simmering water. Beat in the butter or margarine and syrup. Stir in the cereal. Spoon into paper cake cases (cupcake papers) and leave to cool and set.

Nougat Layer Cake

Makes one 900 g/2 lb cake

15 g/½ oz/1 tbsp powdered gelatine

100 ml/3½ fl oz/6½ tbsp water

1 packet trifle sponges

225 g/8 oz/1 cup butter or margarine, softened

50 g/2 oz/¼ cup caster (superfine) sugar

400 g/14 oz/1 large can condensed milk

5 ml/1 tsp lemon juice

5 ml/1 tsp vanilla essence (extract)

5 ml/1 tsp cream of tartar

100 g/4 oz/2/3 cup dried mixed fruit (fruit cake mix), chopped

Sprinkle the gelatine over the water in a small bowl, then stand the bowl in a pan of hot water until the gelatine is transparent. Cool slightly. Line a 900 g/2 lb loaf tin (pan) with foil so that the foil will cover the top of the tin, then arrange half the trifle sponges on the base. Beat together the butter or margarine and sugar until creamy, then beat in all the remaining ingredients. Spoon into the tin and arrange the remaining trifle sponges on top. Cover with foil and put a weight on the top. Chill until firm.

Milk and Nutmeg Squares

Makes 20

For the base:

225 g/8 oz/2 cups plain biscuit (cookie) crumbs

30 ml/2 tbsp soft brown sugar

2.5 ml/½ tsp grated nutmeg

100 g/4 oz/½ cup butter or margarine, melted

For the filling:

1.2 litres/2 pts/5 cups milk

25 g/1 oz/2 tbsp butter or margarine

2 eggs, separated

225 g/8 oz/1 cup caster (superfine) sugar

100 g/4 oz/1 cup cornflour (cornstarch)

50 g/2 oz/½ cup plain (all-purpose) flour

5 ml/1 tsp baking powder

A pinch of grated nutmeg

Grated nutmeg for sprinkling

To make the base, mix the biscuit crumbs, sugar and nutmeg into the melted butter or margarine and press into the base of a greased 30 x 20 cm/12 x 8 in cake tin (pan).

To make the filling, bring 1 litre/ 1¾ pts/4¼ cups of the milk to the boil in a large pan. Add the butter or margarine. Beat the egg yolks with the remaining milk. Mix in the sugar, cornflour, flour, baking powder and nutmeg. Beat a little of the boiling milk into the egg yolk mixture until blended to a paste, then mix the paste into the boiling milk, stirring continuously over a low heat for a few minutes until thickened. Remove from the heat. Beat the egg whites until stiff, then fold them into the mixture. Spoon over the base and sprinkle generously with nutmeg. Leave to cool, then chill and cut into squares before serving.

Muesli Crunch

Makes about 16 squares

400 g/14 oz/3½ cups plain (semi-sweet) chocolate

45 ml/3 tbsp golden (light corn) syrup

25 g/1 oz/2 tbsp butter or margarine

About 225 g/8 oz/2/3 cup muesli

Melt together half the chocolate, the syrup and butter or margarine. Gradually stir in enough muesli to make a stiff mixture. Press into a greased Swiss roll tin (jelly roll pan). Melt the remaining chocolate and smooth over the top. Chill in the fridge before cutting into squares.

Orange Mousse Squares

Makes 20

25 g/1 oz/2 tbsp powdered gelatine

75 ml/5 tbsp cold water

225 g/8 oz/2 cups plain biscuit (cookie) crumbs

50 g/2 oz/¼ cup butter or margarine, melted

400 g/14 oz/1 large can evaporated milk

150 g/5 oz/2/3 cup caster (superfine) sugar

400 ml/14 fl oz/1¾ cups orange juice

Whipped cream and chocolate sweets to decorate

Sprinkle the gelatine over the water in a bowl and leave until spongy. Stand the bowl in a pan of hot water and leave until dissolved. Leave to cool slightly. Stir the biscuit crumbs into the melted butter and press on to the base and sides of a greased 30 x 20 cm/12 x 8 in shallow cake tin (pan). Beat the milk until thick, then gradually beat in the sugar, followed by the dissolved gelatine and the orange juice. Spoon over the base and chill until set. Cut into squares and decorate with piped whipped cream and chocolate sweets.

Peanut Squares

Makes 18

225 g/8 oz/2 cups plain biscuit (cookie) crumbs

100 g/4 oz/½ cup butter or margarine, melted

225 g/8 oz/1 cup crunchy peanut butter

25 g/1 oz/2 tbsp glacé (candied) cherries

25 g/1 oz/3 tbsp currants

Mix together all the ingredients until well blended. Press into a greased 25 cm/12 in baking tin (pan) and chill until firm, then cut into squares.

Peppermint Caramel Cakes

Makes 16

400 g/14 oz/1 large can condensed milk

600 ml/1 pt/2½ cups milk

30 ml/2 tbsp custard powder

225 g/8 oz/2 cups digestive biscuit (Graham cracker) crumbs

100 g/4 oz/1 cup peppermint chocolate, broken into pieces

Place the unopened can of condensed milk in a pan filled with sufficient water to cover the can. Bring to the boil, cover and simmer for 3 hours, topping up with boiling water as necessary. Leave to cool, then open the can and remove the caramel.

Heat 500 ml/17 fl oz/2¼ cups of the milk with the caramel, bring to the boil and stir together until melted. Mix the custard powder to a paste with the remaining milk, then stir it into the pan and continue to simmer until thickened, stirring continuously. Sprinkle half the biscuit crumbs over the base of a greased 20 cm/8 in square cake tin (pan), then spoon half the caramel custard on top and sprinkle with half the chocolate. Repeat the layers, then leave to cool. Chill, then cut into portions to serve.

Rice Cookies

Makes 24

175 g/6 oz/½ cup clear honey

225 g/8 oz/1 cup granulated sugar

60 ml/4 tbsp water

350 g/12 oz/1 box puffed rice cereal

100 g/4 oz/1 cup roasted peanuts

Melt the honey, sugar and water in a large pan, then leave to cool for 5 minutes. Stir in the cereal and peanuts. Roll into balls, place in paper cake cases (cupcake papers) and leave until cool and set.

Rice and Chocolate Toffette

Makes 225 g/8 oz

50 g/2 oz/¼ cup butter or margarine

30 ml/2 tbsp golden (light corn) syrup

30 ml/2 tbsp cocoa (unsweetened chocolate) powder

60 ml/4 tbsp caster (superfine) sugar

50 g/2 oz/½ cup ground rice

Melt the butter and syrup. Stir in the cocoa and sugar until dissolved, then stir in the ground rice. Bring gently to the boil, reduce the heat and simmer gently for 5 minutes, stirring continuously. Spoon into a greased and lined 20 cm/8 in square tin (pan) and leave to cool slightly. Cut into squares, then leave to cool completely before lifting out of the tin.

Almond Paste

Covers the top and sides of one 23 cm/9 in cake

225 g/8 oz/2 cups ground almonds

225 g/8 oz/11/3 cups icing (confectioners') sugar, sifted

225 g/8 oz/1 cup caster (superfine) sugar

2 eggs, lightly beaten

10 ml/2 tsp lemon juice

A few drops of almond essence (extract)

Beat together the almonds and sugars. Gradually blend in the remaining ingredients until you have a smooth paste. Wrap in clingfilm (plastic wrap) and chill before use.

Sugar-free Almond Paste

Covers the top and sides of one 15 cm/6 in cake

100 g/4 oz/1 cup ground almonds

50 g/2 oz/½ cup fructose

25 g/1 oz/¼ cup cornflour (cornstarch)

1 egg, lightly beaten

Blend together all the ingredients until you have a smooth paste. Wrap in clingfilm (plastic wrap) and chill before using.

Royal Icing

Covers the top and sides of one 20 cm/8 in cake

5 ml/1 tsp lemon juice

2 egg whites

450 g/1 lb/22/3 cups icing (confectioners') sugar, sifted

5 ml/1 tsp glycerine (optional)

Mix together the lemon juice and egg whites and gradually beat in the icing sugar until the icing (frosting) is smooth and white and will coat the back of a spoon. A few drops of glycerine will prevent the icing from becoming too brittle. Cover with a damp cloth and leave to stand for 20 minutes to allow any air bubbles to rise to the surface.

Icing of this consistency can be poured on to the cake and smoothed with a knife dipped in hot water. For piping, mix in extra icing sugar so that the icing is stiff enough to stand in peaks.

Sugar-free Icing

Makes enough to cover one 15 cm/6 in cake

50 g/2 oz/½ cup fructose

A pinch of salt

1 egg white

2.5 ml/½ tsp lemon juice

Process the fructose powder in a food processor until it is as fine as icing sugar. Blend in the salt. Transfer to a heatproof bowl and whisk in the egg white and lemon juice. Place the bowl over a pan of gently simmering water and continue to whisk until stiff peaks form. Remove from the heat and whisk until cool.

Fondant Icing

Makes enough to cover one 20 cm/8 in cake

450 g/1 lb/2 cups caster (superfine) or lump sugar

150 ml/¼ pt/2/3 cup water

15 ml/1 tbsp liquid glucose or 2.5 ml/½ tsp cream of tartar

Dissolve the sugar in the water in a large, heavy-based pan over a low heat. Wipe down the sides of the pan with a brush dipped in cold water to prevent crystals forming. Dissolve the cream of tartar in a little water, then stir into the pan. Bring to the boil and boil steadily to 115°C/242°F when a drop of icing forms a soft ball when dropped into cold water. Slowly pour the syrup into a heatproof bowl and leave until a skin forms. Beat the icing with a wooden spoon until it becomes opaque and firm. Knead until smooth. Warm in a heatproof bowl over a pan of hot water to soften, if necessary, before use.

Butter Icing

Makes enough to fill and cover one 20 cm/8 in cake

100 g/4 oz/½ cup butter or margarine, softened

225 g/ 8 oz/11/3 cups icing (confectioners') sugar, sifted

30 ml/2 tbsp milk

Beat the butter or margarine until soft. Gradually beat in the icing sugar and milk until well blended.

Chocolate Butter Icing

Makes enough to fill and cover one 20 cm/8 in cake

30 ml/2 tbsp cocoa (unsweetened chocolate) powder

15 ml/1 tbsp boiling water

100 g/4 oz/½ cup butter or margarine, softened

225 g/8 oz/11/3 cups icing (confectioners') sugar, sifted

15 ml/1 tbsp milk

Mix the cocoa to a paste with the boiling water, then leave to cool. Beat the butter or margarine until soft. Gradually beat in the icing sugar, milk and cocoa mixture until well blended.

White Chocolate Butter Icing

Makes enough to fill and cover one 20 cm/8 in cake

100 g/4 oz/1 cup white chocolate

100 g/4 oz/½ cup butter or margarine, softened

225 g/8 oz/11/3 cups icing (confectioners') sugar, sifted

15 ml/1 tbsp milk

Melt the chocolate in a heatproof bowl set over a pan of gently simmering water, then leave to cool slightly. Beat the butter or margarine until soft. Gradually beat in the icing sugar, milk and chocolate until well blended.

Coffee Butter Icing

Makes enough to fill and cover one 20 cm/8 in cake

100 g/4 oz/½ cup butter or margarine, softened

225 g/ 8 oz/11/3 cups icing (confectioners') sugar, sifted

15 ml/1 tbsp milk

15 ml/1 tbsp coffee essence (extract)

Beat the butter or margarine until soft. Gradually beat in the icing sugar, milk and coffee essence until well blended.

Lemon Butter Icing

Makes enough to fill and cover one 20 cm/8 in cake

100 g/4 oz/½ cup butter or margarine, softened

225 g/ 8 oz/1 1/3 cups icing (confectioners') sugar, sifted

30 ml/2 tbsp lemon juice

Grated rind of 1 lemon

Beat the butter or margarine until soft. Gradually beat in the icing sugar, lemon juice and rind until well blended.

Orange Butter Icing

Makes enough to fill and cover one 20 cm/8 in cake

100 g/4 oz/½ cup butter or margarine, softened

225 g/ 8 oz/11/3 cups icing (confectioners') sugar, sifted

30 ml/2 tbsp orange juice

Grated rind of 1 orange

Beat the butter or margarine until soft. Gradually beat in the icing sugar, orange juice and rind until well blended.

Cream Cheese Icing

Makes enough to cover one 25 cm/9 in cake

75 g/3 oz/1/3 cup cream cheese

30 ml/2 tbsp butter or margarine

350 g/12 oz/2 cups icing (confectioners') sugar, sifted

5 ml/1 tsp vanilla essence (extract)

Beat together the cheese and butter or margarine until light and fluffy. Gradually beat in the icing sugar and vanilla essence until you have a smooth, creamy icing.

Rye Bread with Wheatgerm

Makes one 450 g/1 lb loaf

15 g/½ oz fresh yeast or 20 ml/ 4 tsp dried yeast

5 ml/1 tsp sugar

450 ml/¾ pt/2 cups warm water

350 g/12 oz/3 cups rye flour

225 g/8 oz/2 cups plain (all-purpose) flour

50 g/2 oz/½ cup wheatgerm

10 ml/2 tsp salt

45 ml/3 tbsp black treacle (molasses)

15 ml/1 tbsp oil

Blend the yeast with the sugar and a little of the warm water, then leave in a warm place until frothy. Mix together the flours, wheatgerm and salt and make a well in the centre. Blend in the yeast mixture with the treacle and oil and mix to a soft dough. Turn out on to a floured surface and knead for 10 minutes until smooth and elastic, or process in a food processor. Place in a oiled bowl, cover with oiled clingfilm (plastic wrap) and leave in a warm place for about 1 hour until doubled in size.

Knead again, then shape into a loaf and place on a greased baking (cookie) sheet. Cover with oiled clingfilm and leave to rise until doubled in size.

Bake in a preheated oven at 220°C/ 425°F/gas mark 7 for 15 minutes. Reduce the oven temperature to 190°C/375°F/gas mark 5 and bake for a further 40 minutes until the loaf sounds hollow when tapped on the base.

Sally Lunn

Makes two 450 g/1 lb loaves

500 ml/16 fl oz/2 cups milk

25 g/1 oz/2 tbsp butter or margarine

30 ml/2 tbsp caster (superfine) sugar

10 ml/2 tsp salt

20 ml/4 tsp dried yeast

60 ml/4 tbsp warm water

900 g/2 lb/8 cups strong plain (bread) flour

3 eggs, beaten

Bring the milk almost to a simmer, then add the butter or margarine, sugar and salt and stir well. Leave to cool until lukewarm. Dissolve the yeast in the warm water. Place the flour in a large bowl and mix in the milk, yeast and eggs. Mix to a soft dough and knead until elastic and no longer sticky. Cover with oiled clingfilm (plastic wrap) and leave to rise for 30 minutes.

Knead the dough again, then cover and leave to rise. Knead it a third time, then cover and leave to rise.

Shape the dough and place in two greased 450 g/1 lb loaf tins (pans). Cover and leave to rise until doubled in bulk. Bake in a preheated oven at 190°C/ 375°F/gas mark 5 for 45 minutes until golden on top and the loaves sound hollow when tapped on the base.

Samos Bread

Makes three 450 g/1 lb loaves

15 g/½ oz fresh yeast or 20 ml/ 4 tsp dried yeast

15 ml/1 tbsp malt extract

600 ml/1 pt/2½ cups warm water

25 g/1 oz/2 tbsp vegetable fat (shortening)

900 g/2 lb/8 cups wholemeal (wholewheat) flour

30 ml/2 tbsp milk powder (non-fat dry milk)

10 ml/2 tsp salt

15 ml/1 tbsp clear honey

50 g/2 oz/½ cup sesame seeds, roasted

25 g/1 oz/¼ cup sunflower seeds, roasted

Blend the yeast with the malt extract and a little of the warm water and leave in a warm place for 10 minutes until frothy. Rub the fat into the flour and milk powder, then stir in the salt and make a well in the centre. Pour in the yeast mixture, the remaining warm water and the honey and mix to a dough. Knead well until smooth and elastic. Add the seeds and knead for a further 5 minutes until well blended. Shape into three 450 g/1 lb loaves and place on a greased baking (cookie) sheet. Cover with oiled clingfilm (plastic wrap) and leave in a warm place for 40 minutes until doubled in size.

Bake in a preheated oven at 230°F/ 450°F/gas mark 8 for 30 minutes until golden brown and hollow-sounding when tapped on the base.

Sesame Baps

Makes 12

25 g/1 oz fresh yeast or 40 ml/ 2½ tbsp dried yeast

5 ml/1 tsp caster (superfine) sugar

150 ml/¼ pt/2/3 cup warm milk

450 g/1 lb/4 cups strong plain (bread) flour

5 ml/1 tsp salt

25 g/1 oz/2 tbsp lard (shortening)

150 ml/¼ pt/2/3 cup warm water

30 ml/2 tbsp sesame seeds

Blend the yeast with the sugar and a little of the warm milk and leave in a warm place until frothy. Mix the flour and salt in a bowl, rub in the lard and make a well in the centre. Pour in the yeast mixture, the remaining milk and the water and mix to a soft dough. Turn out on to a floured surface and knead for 10 minutes until smooth and elastic, or process in a food processor. Place in an oiled bowl, cover with oiled clingfilm (plastic wrap) and leave in a warm place for about 1 hour until doubled in size.

Knead again and shape into 12 rolls, flatten them slightly and arrange on a greased baking (cookie) sheet. Cover with oiled clingfilm (plastic wrap) and leave to rise in a warm place for 20 minutes.

Brush with water, sprinkle with seeds and bake in a preheated oven at 220°C/425°F/gas mark 7 for 15 minutes until golden.

Sourdough Starter

Makes about 450 g/1 lb

450 ml/¾ pt/2 cups lukewarm water

25 g/1 oz fresh yeast or 40 ml/ 2½ tbsp dried yeast

225 g/8 oz/2 cups plain (all-purpose) flour

2.5 ml/½ tsp salt

To feed:

225 g/8 oz/2 cups plain (all-purpose) flour

450 ml/¾ pt/2 cups lukewarm water

Mix together the main ingredients in a bowl, cover with muslin (cheesecloth) and leave in a warm place for 24 hours. Add 50 g/2 oz/½ cup plain flour and 120 ml/4 fl oz/½ cup lukewarm water, cover and leave for a further 24 hours. Repeat three times, by which time the mixture should smell sour, then transfer to the fridge. Replace any starter you use with an equal mixture of lukewarm water and flour.

Soda Bread

Makes one 20 cm/8 in loaf

450 g/1 lb/4 cups plain (all-purpose) flour

10 ml/2 tsp bicarbonate of soda (baking soda)

10 ml/2 tsp cream of tartar

5 ml/1 tsp salt

25 g/1 oz/2 tbsp lard (shortening)

5 ml/1 tsp caster (superfine) sugar

15 ml/1 tbsp lemon juice

300 ml/½ pt/1¼ cups milk

Mix together the flour, bicarbonate of soda, cream of tartar and salt. Rub in the lard until the mixture resembles breadcrumbs. Stir in the sugar. Mix the lemon juice into the milk, then stir it into the dry ingredients until you have a soft dough. Knead lightly, then shape the dough into a 20 cm/8 in round and flatten it slightly. Place it on a floured baking tray and mark into quarters with the blade of a knife. Bake in a preheated oven at 200°C/400°F/gas mark 6 for about 30 minutes until crusty on top. Leave to cool before serving.

Sourdough Bread

Makes two 350 g/12 oz loaves

250 ml/8 fl oz/1 cup lukewarm water

15 ml/1 tbsp caster (superfine) sugar

30 ml/2 tbsp melted butter or margarine

15 ml/1 tbsp salt

250 ml/8 fl oz/1 cup Sourdough Starter

2.5 ml/½ tsp bicarbonate of soda (baking soda)

450 g/1 lb/4 cups plain (all-purpose) flour

Mix together the water, sugar, butter or margarine and salt. Mix the sourdough starter with the bicarbonate of soda and stir into the mixture, then beat in the flour to make a stiff dough. Knead the dough until smooth and satiny, adding a little more flour if necessary. Place in an oiled bowl, cover with oiled clingfilm (plastic wrap) and leave in a warm place for about 1 hour until doubled in size.

Knead again lightly and shape into two loaves. Place on a greased baking (cookie) sheet, cover with oiled clingfilm and leave to rise for about 40 minutes until doubled in size.

Bake in a preheated oven at 190°C/ 375°F/gas mark 5 for about 40 minutes until golden brown and hollow-sounding when tapped on the base.

Sourdough Buns

Makes 12

50 g/2 oz/¼ cup butter or margarine

175 g/6 oz/1½ cups plain (all-purpose) flour

5 ml/1 tsp salt

2.5 ml/½ tsp bicarbonate of soda (baking soda)

250 ml/8 fl oz/1 cup Sourdough Starter

A little melted butter or margarine for glazing

Rub the butter or margarine into the flour and salt until the mixture resembles breadcrumbs. Mix the bicarbonate of soda into the starter, then stir it into the flour to make a stiff dough. Knead until smooth and no longer sticky. Shape into small rolls and arrange well apart on a greased baking (cookie) sheet. Brush the tops with butter or margarine, cover with oiled clingfilm (plastic wrap) and leave to rise for about 1 hour until doubled in size. Bake in a preheated oven at 220°C/425°F/gas mark 8 for 15 minutes until golden brown.

Vienna Loaf

Makes one 675 g/1½ lb loaf

15 g/½ oz fresh yeast or 20 ml/ 4 tsp dried yeast

5 ml/1 tsp caster (superfine) sugar

300 ml/½ pt/1¼ cups warm milk

40 g/1½ oz/3 tbsp butter or margarine

450 g/1 lb/4 cups strong plain (bread) flour

5 ml/1 tsp salt

1 egg, well beaten

Blend the yeast with the sugar and a little of the warm milk and leave in a warm place until frothy. Melt the butter or margarine and add the remaining milk. Blend together the yeast mixture, butter mixture, flour, salt and egg to make a soft dough. Knead until smooth and no longer sticky. Place in an oiled bowl, cover with oiled clingfilm (plastic wrap) and leave in a warm place for about 1 hour until doubled in size.

Knead the dough again, then shape into a loaf and place on a greased baking (cookie) sheet. Cover with oiled clingfilm and leave to rise in a warm place for 20 minutes.

Bake in a preheated oven at 230°C/ 450°F/gas mark 8 for 25 minutes until golden and hollow-sounding when tapped on the base.

Wholemeal Bread

Makes two 450 g/1 lb loaves

15 g/½ oz fresh yeast or 20 ml/ 4 tsp dried yeast

5 ml/1 tsp sugar

300 ml/½ pt/1¼ cups warm water

550 g/1¼ lb/5 cups wholemeal (wholewheat) flour

5 ml/1 tsp salt

45 ml/3 tbsp buttermilk

Sesame or caraway seeds for sprinkling (optional)

Blend the yeast with the sugar and a little of the warm water and leave in a warm place for 20 minutes until frothy. Place the flour and salt in a bowl and make a well in the centre. Stir in the yeast, the remaining water and the buttermilk. Work to a firm dough which leaves the sides of the bowl cleanly, adding a little extra flour or water if necessary. Knead on a lightly floured surface or in a processor until elastic and no longer sticky. Shape the dough into two greased 450 g/1 lb loaf tins (pans), cover with oiled clingfilm (plastic wrap) and leave to rise for about 45 minutes until the dough has risen just above the top of the tins.

Sprinkle with sesame or caraway seeds, if using. Bake in a preheated oven at 230°C/450°F/gas mark 8 for 15 minutes, then reduce the oven temperature to 190°C/375°F/gas mark 5 and bake for a further 25 minutes until golden brown and hollow-sounding when tapped on the base.

Wholemeal Honey Bread

Makes one 900 g/2 lb loaf

15 g/½ oz fresh yeast or 20 ml/ 4 tsp dried yeast

450 ml/¾ pt/2 cups warm water

45 ml/3 tbsp set honey

50 g/2 oz/¼ cup butter or margarine

750 g/1½ lb/6 cups wholemeal (wholewheat) flour

2.5 ml/½ tsp salt

15 ml/1 tbsp sesame seeds

Blend the yeast with a little of the water and a little of the honey and leave in a warm place for 20 minutes until frothy. Rub the butter or margarine into the flour and salt, then mix in the yeast mixture and the remaining water and honey until you have a soft dough. Knead until elastic and no longer sticky. Place in an oiled bowl, cover with oiled clingfilm (plastic wrap) and leave in a warm place for about 1 hour until doubled in size.

Knead again and shape into a greased 900 g/2 lb loaf tin (pan). Cover with oiled clingfilm and leave to rise for 20 minutes until the dough comes above the top of the tin.

Bake in a preheated oven at 220°C/ 425°F/gas mark 7 for 15 minutes. Reduce the oven temperature to 190°C/375°F/gas mark 5 and bake for a further 20 minutes until the loaf is golden brown and hollow-sounding when tapped on the base.

Quick Wholemeal Rolls

Makes 12

20 ml/4 tsp dried yeast

375 ml/13 fl oz/1½ cups warm water

50 g/2 oz/¼ cup soft brown sugar

100 g/4 oz/1 cup wholemeal (wholewheat) flour

100 g/4 oz/1 cup plain (all-purpose) flour

5 ml/1 tsp salt

Blend the yeast with the water and a little sugar and leave in a warm place until frothy. Stir into the flours and salt with the remaining sugar and mix to a soft dough. Spoon the dough into muffin tins (pans) and leave to rise for 20 minutes until the dough has risen to the top of the tins.

Bake in a preheated oven at 180°C/ 350°F/gas mark 4 for 30 minutes until well risen and golden brown.

Wholemeal Bread with Walnuts

Makes one 900 g/2 lb loaf

15 g/½ oz fresh yeast or 20 ml/ 4 tsp dried yeast

5 ml/1 tsp soft brown sugar

450 ml/¾ pt/2 cups warm water

450 g/1 lb/4 cups wholemeal (wholewheat) flour

175 g/6 oz/1½ cups strong plain (bread) flour

5 ml/1 tsp salt

15 ml/1 tbsp walnut oil

100 g/4 oz/1 cup walnuts, coarsely chopped

Blend the yeast with the sugar and a little of the warm water and leave in a warm place for 20 minutes until frothy. Mix the flours and salt in a bowl, add the yeast mixture, the oil and the remaining warm water and mix to a firm dough. Knead until smooth and no longer sticky. Place in an oiled bowl, cover with oiled clingfilm (plastic wrap) and leave in a warm place for about 1 hour until doubled in size.

Knead again lightly and work in the nuts, then shape into a greased 900 g/2 lb loaf tin (pan), cover with oiled clingfilm and leave in a warm place for 30 minutes until the dough has risen above the top of the tin.

Bake in a preheated oven at 220°C/ 425°F/gas mark 7 for 30 minutes until golden brown and hollow-sounding when tapped on the base.

Almond Plait

Makes one 450 g/1 lb loaf

15 g/½ oz fresh yeast or 20 ml/ 4 tsp dried yeast

40 g/1½ oz/3 tbsp caster (superfine) sugar

100 ml/3½ fl oz/6½ tbsp warm milk

350 g/12 oz/3 cups strong plain (bread) flour

2.5 ml/½ tsp salt

50 g/2 oz/¼ cup butter or margarine, melted

1 egg

For the filling and glaze:

50 g/2 oz Almond Paste

45 ml/3 tbsp apricot jam (conserve)

50g /2 oz/1/3 cup raisins

50 g/2 oz/½ cup chopped almonds

1 egg yolk

Blend the yeast with 5 ml/1 tsp of the sugar and a little of the milk and leave in a warm place for 20 minutes until frothy. Mix the flour and salt in a bowl and make a well in the centre. Mix in the yeast mixture, the remaining sugar and milk, the melted butter or margarine and the egg and mix to a smooth dough. Knead until elastic and no longer sticky. Place in an oiled bowl, cover with oiled clingfilm (plastic wrap) and leave in a warm place for about 1 hour until doubled in size.

Roll out the dough on a lightly floured surface to a 30 x 40 cm/12 x 16 in rectangle. Mix together the filling ingredients except the egg yolk and work until smooth, then spread down the centre one-third of the dough. Cut slashes in the outside two-thirds of the dough from the edges at an angle towards the filling at about 2 cm/¾ in intervals. Fold alternate left and right strips over the filling and seal the ends together firmly. Place on a greased baking (cookie) sheet, cover and leave in a warm place for 30 minutes until doubled in size. Brush with egg yolk and bake in a preheated oven at 190°C/375°F/gas mark 5 for 30 minutes until golden brown.

Brioches

Makes 12

15 g/½ oz fresh yeast or 20 ml/ 4 tsp dried yeast

30 ml/2 tbsp warm water

2 eggs, lightly beaten

225 g/8 oz/2 cups strong plain (bread) flour

15 ml/1 tbsp caster (superfine) sugar

2.5 ml/½ tsp salt

50 g/2 oz/¼ cup butter or margarine, melted

Mix together the yeast, water and eggs, then stir into the flour, sugar, salt and butter or margarine and mix to a soft dough. Knead until elastic and no longer sticky. Place in an oiled bowl, cover and leave in a warm place for about 1 hour until doubled in size.

Knead again, divide into 12 pieces, then break a small ball off each piece. Shape the larger pieces into balls and place in 7.5 cm/ 3 in fluted brioche or muffin tins (pans). Press a finger right through the dough, then press the remaining balls of dough on the top. Cover and leave in a warm place for about 30 minutes until the dough has reached just above the tops of the tins.

Bake in a preheated oven at 230°C/ 450°F/gas mark 8 for 10 minutes until golden.

Plaited Brioche

Makes one 675 g/1½ lb loaf

25 g/1 oz fresh yeast or 40 ml/ 2½ tbsp dried yeast

5 ml/1 tsp caster (superfine) sugar

250 ml/8 fl oz/1 cup warm milk

675 g/1½ lb/6 cups strong plain (bread) flour

5 ml/1 tsp salt

1 egg, beaten

150 ml/¼ pt/2/3 cup warm water

1 egg yolk

Blend the yeast with the sugar with a little of the warm milk and leave in a warm place for 20 minutes until frothy. Mix the flour and salt and make a well in the centre. Add the egg, the yeast mixture, the remaining warm milk and enough of the warm water to mix to a soft dough. Knead until soft and no longer sticky. Place in an oiled bowl, cover with oiled clingfilm (plastic wrap) and leave in a warm place for about 1 hour until doubled in size.

Knead the dough lightly, then divide into quarters. Roll three pieces into thin strips about 38 cm/15 in long. Moisten one end of each strip and press them together, then plait the strips together, moisten and fasten the ends. Place on a greased baking (cookie) sheet. Divide the remaining piece of dough into three, roll out into 38 cm/15 in strips and plait together in the same way to make a thinner plait. Beat the egg yolk with 15 ml/1 tbsp of water and brush over the large plait. Gently press the smaller plait on top and brush with the egg glaze. Cover and leave in a warm place to rise for 40 minutes.

Bake in a preheated oven at 200°C/ 400°F/gas mark 6 for 45 minutes until golden brown and hollow-sounding when tapped on the base.

Apple Brioches

Makes 12

For the dough:

15 g/½ oz fresh yeast or 10 ml/ 2 tsp dried yeast

75 ml/5 tbsp warm milk

100 g/4 oz/1 cup wholemeal (wholewheat) flour

350 g/12 oz/3 cups strong plain (bread) flour

30 ml/2 tbsp clear honey

4 eggs

A pinch of salt

200 g/7 oz/scant 1 cup butter or margarine, melted

For the filling:

75 g/3 oz apple purée (sauce)

25 g/1 oz/¼ cup wholemeal (wholewheat) breadcrumbs

25 g/3 oz/½ cup sultanas (golden raisins)

2.5 ml/½ tsp ground cinnamon

1 egg, beaten

To make the dough, blend the yeast with the warm milk and wholemeal flour and leave in a warm place for 20 minutes to ferment. Add the plain flour, honey, eggs and salt and knead well. Pour on the melted butter or margarine and continue to knead until the dough is elastic and smooth. Place in an oiled bowl, cover with oiled clingfilm (plastic wrap) and leave in a warm place for about 1 hour until doubled in size.

Mix together all the filling ingredients except the egg. Shape the dough into 12 pieces, then take one-third off each piece. Shape the larger pieces to fit greased fluted brioche or muffin tins (pans). Press a large hole almost through to the base with a finger or fork handle and fill with the filling. Shape each of the smaller dough pieces into a ball, moisten the top of the dough and press over the filling to seal it into the brioche. Cover and leave in a warm place for 40 minutes until almost doubled in size.

Brush with beaten egg and bake in a preheated oven at 220°C/425°F/gas mark 7 for 15 minutes until golden.

Tofu and Nut Brioches

Makes 12

For the dough:

15 g/½ oz fresh yeast or 20 ml/ 4 tsp dried yeast

75 ml/5 tbsp warm milk

100 g/4 oz/1 cup wholemeal (wholewheat) flour

350 g/12 oz/3 cups strong plain (bread) flour

30 ml/2 tsp clear honey

4 eggs

A pinch of salt

200 g/7 oz/scant 1 cup butter or margarine, melted

For the filling:

50 g/2 oz/¼ cup tofu, diced

25 g/1 oz/¼ cup cashew nuts, toasted and chopped

25 g/1 oz chopped mixed vegetables

½ onion, chopped

1 garlic clove, chopped

2.5 ml/½ tsp dried mixed herbs

2.5 ml/½ tsp French mustard

1 egg, beaten

To make the dough, blend the yeast with the warm milk and wholemeal flour and leave in a warm place for 20 minutes to ferment. Add the plain flour, honey, eggs and salt and knead well. Pour on the melted butter or margarine and continue to knead until the dough is elastic and smooth. Place in an oiled bowl, cover with oiled clingfilm (plastic wrap) and leave in a warm place for about 1 hour until doubled in size.

Mix together all the filling ingredients except the egg. Shape the dough into 12 pieces, then take one-third off each piece. Shape the larger pieces to fit greased fluted brioche or muffin tins (pans). Press a large hole almost through to the base with a finger or fork handle and fill with the filling. Shape each of the smaller dough pieces into a ball, moisten the top of the dough and press over the filling to seal it into the brioche. Cover and leave in a warm place for 40 minutes until almost doubled in size.

Brush with beaten egg and bake in a preheated oven at 220°C/425°F/gas mark 7 for 15 minutes until golden.

Chelsea Buns

Makes 9

225 g/8 oz/2 cups strong plain (bread) flour

5 ml/1 tsp caster (superfine) sugar

15 g/½ oz fresh yeast or 20 ml/ 4 tsp dried yeast

120 ml/4 fl oz/½ cup warm milk

A pinch of salt

15 g/½ oz/1 tbsp butter or margarine

1 egg, beaten

For the filling:

75 g/3 oz/½ cup mixed dried fruit (fruit cake mix)

25 g/1 oz/3 tbsp chopped mixed (candied) peel

50 g/2 oz/¼ cup soft brown sugar

A little clear honey for glazing

Mix together 50 g/2 oz/¼ cup of the flour, the caster sugar, yeast and a little of the milk and leave in a warm place for 20 minutes until frothy. Mix together the remaining flour and salt and rub in the butter or margarine. Blend in the egg, the yeast mixture and the remaining warm milk and mix to a dough. Knead until elastic and no longer sticky. Place in an oiled bowl, cover with oiled clingfilm (plastic wrap) and leave in a warm place for about 1 hour until doubled in size.

Knead again and roll out to a 33 x 23 cm/13 x 9 in rectangle. Mix together all the filling ingredients except the honey and spread over the dough. Roll up from one long side and seal the edge with a little water. Cut the roll into nine equal-sized pieces and place in a lightly greased baking tin (pan). Cover and leave in a warm place for 30 minutes until doubled in size.

Bake in a preheated oven at 190°C/ 375°F/gas mark 5 for 25 minutes until golden brown. Remove from the oven and brush with honey, then leave to cool.

Coffee Buns

Makes 16

225 g/8 oz/1 cup butter or margarine

450 g/1 lb/4 cups wholemeal (wholewheat) flour

20 ml/4 tsp baking powder

5 ml/1 tsp salt

225 g/8 oz/1 cup soft brown sugar

2 eggs, lightly beaten

100 g/4 oz/2/3 cup currants

5 ml/1 tsp instant coffee powder

15 ml/1 tbsp hot water

75 ml/5 tbsp clear honey

Rub the butter or margarine into the flour, baking powder and salt until the mixture resembles breadcrumbs. Stir in the sugar. Beat in the eggs to make a soft but not sticky dough, then mix in the currants. Dissolve the coffee powder in the hot water and add to the dough. Shape into 16 flattened balls and place, well apart, on a greased baking (cookie) sheet. Press a finger into the centre of each bun and add a teaspoonful of honey. Bake in a preheated oven at 220°C/425°F/gas mark 7 for 10 minutes until light and golden brown.

Crème Fraîche Bread

Makes two 450 g/1 lb loaves

25 g/1 oz fresh yeast or 40 ml/ 2½ tbsp dried yeast

75 g/3 oz/1/3 cup soft brown sugar

60 ml/4 tbsp warm water

60 ml/4 tbsp crème fraîche, at room temperature

350 g/12 oz/3 cups plain (all-purpose) flour

5 ml/1 tsp salt

A pinch of grated nutmeg

3 eggs

50 g/2 oz/¼ cup butter or margarine

A little milk and sugar for glazing

Blend the yeast with 5 ml/1 tsp of the sugar and the warm water and leave in a warm place for 20 minutes until frothy. Stir the crème fraîche into the yeast. Place the flour, salt and nutmeg in a bowl and make a well in the centre. Mix in the yeast mixture, eggs and butter and work to a soft dough. Knead until smooth and elastic. Place in an oiled bowl, cover with oiled clingfilm (plastic wrap) and leave in a warm place for about 1 hour until doubled in size.

Knead the dough again, then shape into two 450 g/1 lb loaf tins (pans). Cover and leave in a warm place for 35 minutes until doubled in size.

Brush the top of the loaves with a little milk, then sprinkle with sugar. Bake in a preheated oven at 180°C/350°F/gas mark 4 for 30 minutes. Leave to cool in the tin for 10 minutes, then turn out on to a wire rack to finish cooling.

Croissants

Makes 12

25 g/1 oz/2 tbsp lard (shortening)

450 g/1 lb/4 cups strong plain (bread) flour

2.5 ml/½ tsp caster (superfine) sugar

10 ml/2 tsp salt

25 g/1 oz fresh yeast or 40 ml/ 2½ tbsp dried yeast

250 ml/8 fl oz/1 cup warm water

2 eggs, lightly beaten

100 g/4 oz/½ cup butter or margarine, diced

Rub the lard into the flour, sugar and salt until the mixture resembles breadcrumbs, then make a well in the centre. Mix the yeast with the water, and add to the flour with one of the eggs. Work the mixture together until you have a soft dough that leaves the sides of the bowl cleanly. Turn out on to a lightly floured surface and knead until smooth and no longer sticky. Roll out the dough to a 20 x 50 cm/8 x 20 in strip. Dot the top two-thirds of the dough with one-third of the butter or margarine, leaving a thin gap round the edge. Fold the unbuttered part of the dough up over the next one-third, then fold the top one-third down over that. Press the edges together to seal, and give the dough a quarter turn so the folded edge is on your left. Repeat the process with the next one-third of the butter or margarine, fold and repeat once more so that you have used all the fat. Put the folded dough in an oiled polythene bag and chill for 30 minutes.

Roll, fold and turn the dough again three more times without adding any more fat. Return to the bag and chill for 30 minutes.

Roll out the dough to a 40 x 38 cm/ 16 x 15 in rectangle, trim the edges and cut into 12 15 cm/6 in triangles. Brush the triangles with a little beaten egg and roll up from the base, then curve into crescent shapes and place, well apart, on a greased baking (cookie) sheet. Brush the tops with egg, cover and leave in a warm place for about 30 minutes.

Brush the tops with egg again, then bake in a preheated oven at 230°C/425°F/ gas mark 7 for 15–20 minutes until golden and puffy.

Wholemeal Sultana Croissants

Makes 12

25 g/1 oz/2 tbsp lard (shortening)

225 g/8 oz/2 cups strong plain (bread) flour

225 g/8 oz/2 cups wholemeal (wholewheat) flour

10 ml/2 tsp salt

25 g/1 oz fresh yeast or 40 ml/ 2½ tbsp dried yeast

300 ml/½ pt/1¼ cups warm water

2 eggs, lightly beaten

100 g/4 oz/½ cup butter or margarine, diced

45 ml/3 tbsp sultanas (golden raisins)

2.5 ml/½ tsp caster (superfine) sugar

Rub the lard into the flour and salt until the mixture resembles breadcrumbs, then make a well in the centre. Mix the yeast with the water, and add to the flour with one of the eggs. Work the mixture together until you have a soft dough that leaves the sides of the bowl cleanly. Turn out on to a lightly floured surface and knead until smooth and no longer sticky. Roll out the dough to a 20 x 50 cm/8 x 20 in strip. Dot the top two-thirds of the dough with one-third of the butter or margarine, leaving a thin gap round the edge. Fold the unbuttered part of the dough up over the next one-third, then fold the top one-third down over that. Press the edges together to seal, and give the dough a quarter turn so the folded edge is on your left. Repeat the process with the next one-third of the butter or margarine, fold and repeat once more so that you have used all the fat. Put the folded dough in an oiled polythene bag and chill for 30 minutes.

Roll, fold and turn the dough again three more times without adding any more fat. Return to the bag and chill for 30 minutes.

Roll out the dough to a 40 x 38 cm/ 16 x 15 in rectangle, trim the edges and cut into twelve 15 cm/6 in triangles. Brush the triangles with a little beaten egg, sprinkle with sultanas and sugar and roll up from the base, then curve into crescent shapes and place well apart on a greased baking (cookie) sheet. Brush the tops with egg, cover and leave in a warm place for 30 minutes.

Brush the tops with egg again, then bake in a preheated oven at 230°C/425°F/ gas mark 7 for 15–20 minutes until golden and puffy.

Forest Rounds

Makes three 350 g/12 oz loaves

450 g/1 lb/4 cups wholemeal (wholewheat) flour

20 ml/4 tsp baking powder

45 ml/3 tbsp carob powder

5 ml/1 tsp salt

50 g/2 oz/½ cup ground hazelnuts

50 g/2 oz/½ cup chopped mixed nuts

75 g/3 oz/1/3 cup vegetable fat (shortening)

75 g/3 oz/¼ cup clear honey

300 ml/½ pt/1¼ cups milk

2.5 ml/½ tsp vanilla essence (extract)

1 egg, beaten

Mix together the dry ingredients, then rub in the vegetable fat. Dissolve the honey in the milk and vanilla essence and mix into the dry ingredients until you have a soft dough. Shape into three rounds and press to flatten slightly. Cut each loaf partly through into six portions and brush with beaten egg. Place on a greased baking (cookie) sheet and bake in a preheated oven at 230°C/450°F/gas mark 8 for 20 minutes until well risen and golden brown.

Nutty Twist

Makes one 450 g/1 lb loaf

For the dough:
15 g/½ oz fresh yeast or 20 ml/ 4 tsp dried yeast

40 g/1½ oz/3 tbsp caster (superfine) sugar

100 ml/3½ fl oz/6 ½ tbsp warm milk

350 g/12 oz/3 cups strong plain (bread) flour

2.5 ml/½ tsp salt

50 g/2 oz/¼ cup butter or margarine, melted

1 egg

For the filling and glaze:
100 g/4 oz/1 cup ground almonds

2 egg whites

50 g/2 oz/¼ cup caster (superfine) sugar

2.5 ml/½ tsp ground cinnamon

100 g/4 oz/1 cup ground hazelnuts

1 egg yolk

To make the dough, blend the yeast with 5 ml/1 tsp of the sugar and a little of the milk and leave in a warm place for 20 minutes until frothy. Mix the flour and salt in a bowl and make a well in the centre. Mix in the yeast mixture, the remaining sugar and milk, the melted butter or margarine and the egg and mix to a smooth dough. Knead until elastic and no longer sticky. Place in an oiled bowl, cover with oiled clingfilm (plastic wrap) and leave in a warm place for about 1 hour until doubled in size.

Roll out the dough on a lightly floured surface to a 30 x 40 cm/12 x 16 in rectangle. Mix together the filling ingredients, except the egg yolk, until you have a smooth paste, then spread over the dough, just short of the edges. Brush the edges with a little of the egg yolk, then roll up the dough from the long side. Cut the dough exactly in half lengthways, then twist the two pieces together, sealing the ends. Place on a greased baking (cookie) sheet, cover and leave in a warm place for 30 minutes until doubled in size. Brush with egg yolk and bake in a preheated oven at 190°C/375°F/gas mark 5 for 30 minutes until golden brown.

Orange Buns

Makes 24

For the dough:

25 g/1 oz fresh yeast or 40 ml/ 2½ tbsp dried yeast

120 ml/4 fl oz/½ cup warm water

75 g/3 oz/1/3 cup caster (superfine) sugar

100 g/4 oz/½ cup lard (shortening), diced

5 ml/1 tsp salt

250 ml/8 fl oz/1 cup warm milk

60 ml/4 tbsp orange juice

30 ml/2 tbsp grated orange rind

2 eggs, beaten

675 g/1½ lb/6 cups strong plain (bread) flour

For the icing (frosting):

250 g/9 oz/1½ cups icing (confectioners') sugar

5 ml/1 tsp grated orange rind

30 ml/2 tbsp orange juice

To make the dough, dissolve the yeast in the warm water with 5 ml/1 tsp of the sugar and leave until frothy. Mix the lard into the remaining sugar and the salt. Stir in the milk, orange juice, rind and eggs, then blend in the yeast mixture. Gradually add the flour and mix to a firm dough. Knead well. Place in a greased bowl, cover with oiled clingfilm (plastic wrap) and leave in a warm place for about 1 hour until doubled in size.

Roll out to about 2 cm/¾ in thick and cut into rounds with a biscuit (cookie) cutter. Place a little way apart on a greased baking (cookie) sheet and leave in a warm place 25 minutes. Leave to cool.

To make the icing, place the sugar in a bowl and mix in the orange rind. Gradually mix in the orange juice until you have a firm icing. Spoon over the buns when cool and leave to set.

Pain Chocolat

Makes 12

25 g/1 oz/2 tbsp lard (shortening)

450 g/1 lb/4 cups strong plain (bread) flour

2.5 ml/½ tsp caster (superfine) sugar

10 ml/2 tsp salt

25 g/1 oz fresh yeast or 40 ml/ 2½ tbsp dried yeast

250 ml/8 fl oz/1 cup warm water

2 eggs, lightly beaten

100 g/4 oz/½ cup butter or margarine, diced

100 g/4 oz/1 cup plain (semi-sweet) chocolate, broken into 12 pieces

Rub the lard into the flour, sugar and salt until the mixture resembles breadcrumbs, then make a well in the centre. Mix the yeast with the water, and add to the flour with one of the eggs. Work the mixture together until you have a soft dough which leaves the sides of the bowl cleanly. Turn out on to a lightly floured surface and knead until smooth and no longer sticky. Roll out the dough to a 20 x 50 cm/8 x 20 in strip. Dot the top two-thirds of the dough with one-third of the butter or margarine, leaving a thin gap round the edge. Fold the unbuttered part of the dough up over the next one-third, then fold the top one-third down over that, Press the edges together to seal, and give the dough a quarter turn so the folded edge is on your left. Repeat the process with the next one-third of the butter or margarine, fold and repeat once more so that you have used all the fat. Put the folded dough in an oiled polythene bag and chill for 30 minutes.

Roll, fold and turn the dough again three more times without adding any more fat. Return to the bag and chill for 30 minutes.

Divide the dough into 12 pieces and roll out into rectangles about 5 cm/2 in wide and 5 mm/¼ in thick. Place a piece of chocolate in the centre of each and roll up, enclosing the chocolate. Place well apart on a greased baking (cookie) sheet. Brush the tops with egg, cover and leave in a warm place for 30 minutes.

Brush the tops with egg again, then bake in a preheated oven at 230°C/425°F/ gas mark 7 for 15–20 minutes until golden and puffy.

Pandolce

Makes two 675 g/1½ lb loaves

175 g/6 oz/1 cup raisins

45 ml/3 tbsp Marsala or sweet sherry

25 g/1 oz fresh yeast or 40 ml/2½ tbsp dried yeast

175 g/6 oz/¾ cup caster (superfine) sugar

400 ml/14 fl oz/1¾ cups warm milk

900 g/2 lb/8 cups plain (all-purpose) flour

A pinch of salt

45 ml/3 tbsp orange flower water

75 g/3 oz/1/3 cup butter or margarine, melted

50 g/2 oz/½ cup pine nuts

50 g/2 oz/½ cup pistachio nuts

10 ml/2 tsp crushed fennel seeds

50 g/2 oz/1/3 cup crystallised (candied) lemon rind, chopped

Grated rind of 1 orange

Mix the raisins and Marsala and leave to soak. Blend the yeast with 5 ml/ 1 tsp of the sugar and a little of the warm milk and leave in a warm place for 20 minutes until frothy. Mix the flour, salt and remaining sugar in a bowl and make a well in the centre. Mix in the yeast mixture, the remaining warm milk and the orange flower water. Add the melted butter or margarine and mix to a soft dough. Knead on a lightly floured surface until elastic and no longer sticky. Place in an oiled bowl, cover with oiled clingfilm (plastic wrap) and leave in a warm place for about 1 hour until doubled in size.

Press or roll out the dough on a lightly floured surface to about 1 cm/½ in thick. Sprinkle with the raisins, nuts, fennel seeds, lemon and orange rinds. Roll up the dough, then press or roll out and roll up again. Shape into a round and place on a greased baking (cookie) sheet. Cover with oiled clingfilm and leave in a warm place for about 1 hour until doubled in size.

Make a triangular cut on the top of the loaf, then bake in a preheated oven at 190°C/375°F/gas mark 5 for 20 minutes. Reduce the oven temperature to 160°C/325°F/gas mark 3 and bake for a further 1 hour until golden and hollow-sounding when tapped on the base.

Panettone

Makes one 23 cm/9 in cake

40 g/1½ oz fresh yeast or 60 ml/ 4 tbsp dried yeast

150 g/5 oz/2/3 cup caster (superfine) sugar

300 ml/½ pt/1¼ cups warm milk

225 g/8 oz/1 cup butter or margarine, melted

5 ml/1 tsp salt

Grated rind of 1 lemon

A pinch of grated nutmeg

6 egg yolks

675 g/1½ lb/6 cups strong plain (bread) flour

175 g/6 oz/1 cup raisins

175 g/6 oz/1 cup chopped mixed (candied) peel

75 g/3 oz/¼ cup almonds, chopped

Blend the yeast with 5 ml/1 tsp of the sugar with a little of the warm milk and leave in a warm place for 20 minutes until frothy. Mix the melted butter with the remaining sugar, the salt, lemon rind, nutmeg and egg yolks. Stir the mixture into the flour with the yeast mixture and blend to a smooth dough. Knead until no longer sticky. Place in an oiled bowl, cover with oiled clingfilm (plastic wrap) and leave in a warm place for 20 minutes. Mix together the raisins, mixed peel and almonds and work into the dough. Cover again and leave in a warm place for a further 30 minutes.

Knead the dough lightly, then shape into a greased and lined 23 cm/9 in deep cake tin (pan). Cover and leave in a warm place for 30 minutes until the dough rises well above the top of the tin. Bake in a preheated oven at 190°C/375°F/gas mark 5 for 1½ hours until a skewer inserted in the centre comes out clean.

Apple and Date Loaf

Makes one 900 g/2 lb loaf

350 g/12 oz/3 cups self-raising (self-rising) flour

50 g/2 oz/¼ cup soft brown sugar

5 ml/1 tsp mixed (apple-pie) spice

5 ml/1 tsp ground cinnamon

2.5 ml/½ tsp grated nutmeg

A pinch of salt

1 large cooking (tart) apple, peeled, cored and chopped

175 g/6 oz/1 cup stoned (pitted) dates, chopped

Grated rind of ½ lemon

2 eggs, lightly beaten

150 ml/¼ pt/2/3 cup plain yoghurt

Mix together the dry ingredients, then stir in the apple, dates and lemon rind. Make a well in the centre, add the eggs and yoghurt and gradually mix to a dough. Turn out on to a lightly floured surface and shape into a greased and floured 900 g/2 lb loaf tin (pan). Bake in a preheated oven at 160°C/325°F/gas mark 3 for 1½ hours until well risen and golden brown. Leave to cool in the tin for 5 minutes, then turn out on to a wire rack to finish cooling.

Apple and Sultana Bread

Makes three 350 g/12 oz loaves

25 g/1 oz fresh yeast or 40 ml/2½ tbsp dried yeast

10 ml/2 tsp malt extract

375 ml/13 fl oz/1½ cups warm water

450 g/1 lb/4 cups wholemeal (wholewheat) flour

5 ml/1 tsp soya flour

50 g/2 oz/½ cup rolled oats

2.5 ml/½ tsp salt

25 g/1 oz/2 tbsp soft brown sugar

15 ml/1 tbsp lard (shortening)

225 g/8 oz cooking (tart) apples, peeled, cored and chopped

400 g/14 oz/21/3 cups sultanas (golden raisins)

2.5 ml/½ tsp ground cinnamon

1 egg, beaten

Blend the yeast with the malt extract and a little of the warm water and leave in a warm place until frothy. Mix together the flour, oats, salt and sugar, rub in the lard and make a well in the centre. Mix in the yeast mixture and the remaining warm water and knead to a smooth dough. Mix in the apples, sultanas and cinnamon. Knead until elastic and no longer sticky. Place the dough in an oiled bowl and cover with oiled clingfilm (plastic wrap). Leave in a warm place for 1 hour until doubled in size.

Knead the dough lightly, then shape into three rounds and flatten slightly, then place on a greased baking (cookie) sheet. Brush the tops with beaten egg and bake in a preheated oven at 230°C/450°F/gas mark 8 for 35 minutes until well risen and hollow-sounding when tapped on the base.

Apple and Cinnamon Surprises

Makes 10

For the dough:

25 g/1 oz fresh yeast or 40 ml/2½ tbsp dried yeast

75 g/3 oz/1/3 cup soft brown sugar

300 ml/½ pt/1¼ cups warm water

450 g/1 lb/4 cups wholemeal (wholewheat) flour

2.5 ml/½ tsp salt

25 g/1 oz/¼ cup milk powder (non-fat dry milk)

5 ml/1 tsp ground mixed (apple-pie) spice

5 ml/1 tsp ground cinnamon

75 g/3 oz/1/3 cup butter or margarine

15 ml/1 tbsp grated orange rind

1 egg

For the filling:

450 g/1 lb cooking (tart) apples, peeled, cored and coarsely chopped

75 g/3 oz/½ cup sultanas (golden raisins)

5 ml/1 tsp ground cinnamon

For the glaze:

15 ml/1 tbsp clear honey

30 ml/2 tbsp caster (superfine) sugar

To make the dough, blend the yeast with a little of the sugar and a little of the warm water and leave in a warm place for 20 minutes until frothy. Mix together the flour, salt, milk powder and spices. Rub in the butter or margarine, then stir in the orange rind and make a well in the centre. Add the yeast mixture, the remaining warm water and the egg and mix to a smooth dough. Place in an oiled bowl, cover with oiled clingfilm (plastic wrap) and leave in a warm place for 1 hour until doubled in size.

To make the filling, cook the apples and sultanas in a pan with the cinnamon and a little water until soft and puréed.

Shape the dough into 10 rolls, press your finger into the centre and spoon in some of the filling, then close the dough around the filling. Arrange on a greased baking (cookie) sheet, Cover with oiled clingfilm and leave in a warm place for 40 minutes. Bake in a preheated oven at 230°C/450°F/gas mark 8 for 15 minutes until well risen. Brush with the honey, sprinkle with the sugar and leave to cool.

Apricot Tea Bread

Makes one 900 g/2 lb loaf

225 g/8 oz/2 cups self-raising (self-rising) flour

100 g/4 oz/2/3 cup dried apricots

50 g/2 oz/½ cup almonds, chopped

50 g/2 oz/¼ cup soft brown sugar

50 g/2 oz/¼ cup butter or margarine

100 g/4 oz/1/3 cup golden (light corn) syrup

1 egg

75 ml/5 tbsp milk

Soak the apricots in hot water for 1 hour, then drain and chop.

Mix together the flour, apricots, almonds and sugar. Melt the butter or margarine and syrup. Add to the dry ingredients with the egg and milk. Spoon into a greased and lined 900 g/2 lb loaf tin (pan) and bake in a preheated oven at 180°C/350°F/gas mark 4 for 1 hour until golden brown and firm to the touch.

Apricot and Orange Loaf

Makes one 900 g/2 lb loaf

175 g/6 oz/1 cup no-need-to-soak dried apricots, chopped

150 ml/¼ pt/2/3 cup orange juice

400 g/14 oz/3½ cups plain (all-purpose) flour

175 g/6 oz/¾ cup caster (superfine) sugar

100 g/4 oz/2/3 cup raisins

7.5 ml/1½ tsp baking powder

2.5 ml/½ tsp bicarbonate of soda (baking soda)

2.5 ml/½ tsp salt

Grated rind of 1 orange

1 egg, lightly beaten

25 g/1 oz/2 tbsp butter or margarine, melted

Soak the apricots in the orange juice. Place the dry ingredients and orange rind in a bowl and make a well in the centre. Mix in the apricots and orange juice, egg and melted butter or margarine and work to a stiff mixture. Spoon into a greased and lined 900 g/2 lb loaf tin (pan) and bake in a preheated oven at 180°C/350°F/gas mark 4 for 1 hour until golden and firm to the touch.

Apricot and Walnut Loaf

Makes one 900 g/2 lb loaf

15 g/½ oz fresh yeast or 20 ml/4 tsp dried yeast

30 ml/2 tbsp clear honey

300 ml/½ pt/1¼ cups warm water

25 g/1 oz/2 tbsp butter or margarine

225 g/8 oz/2 cups wholemeal (wholewheat) flour

225 g/8 oz/2 cups plain (all-purpose) flour

5 ml/1 tsp salt

75 g/3 oz/¾ cup walnuts, chopped

175 g/6 oz/1 cup ready-to-eat dried apricots, chopped

Blend the yeast with a little of the honey and a little of the water and leave in a warm place for 20 minutes until frothy. Rub the butter or margarine into the flours and salt and make a well in the centre. Mix in the yeast mixture and the remaining honey and water and mix to a dough. Mix in the walnuts and apricots and knead until smooth and no longer sticky. Place in an oiled bowl, cover and leave in a warm place for 1 hour until doubled in size.

Knead the dough again and shape into a greased 900 g/2 lb loaf tin (pan). Cover with oiled clingfilm (plastic wrap) and leave in a warm place for about 20 minutes until the dough has risen just above the top of the tin. Bake in a preheated oven at 220°C/425°F/gas mark 7 for 30 minutes until golden brown and hollow-sounding when tapped on the base.

Autumn Crown

Makes one large ring loaf

For the dough:

450 g/1 lb/4 cups wholemeal (wholewheat) flour

20 ml/4 tsp baking powder

75 g/3 oz/1/3 cup soft brown sugar

5 ml/1 tsp salt

2.5 ml/½ tsp ground mace

75 g/3 oz/1/3 cup vegetable fat (shortening)

3 egg whites

300 ml/½ pt/1¼ cups milk

For the filling:

175 g/6 oz/1½ cups wholemeal (wholewheat) cake crumbs

50 g/2 oz/½ cup ground hazelnuts or almonds

50 g/2 oz/¼ cup soft brown sugar

75 g/3 oz/½ cup crystallised (candied) ginger, chopped

30 ml/2 tbsp rum or brandy

1 egg, lightly beaten

To glaze:

15 ml/1 tbsp honey

To make the dough, mix together the dry ingredients and rub in the fat. Blend together the egg whites and milk and combine with the mixture until you have a soft, pliable dough.

Mix together the filling ingredients, using just enough of the egg to make a spreading consistency. Roll out the dough on a lightly floured surface to a 20 x 30 cm/8 x 10 in rectangle. Spread the filling over all but the top 2.5 cm/1 in along the long edge. Roll up from the opposite edge, like a Swiss (jelly) roll, and moisten the plain strip of dough to seal. Moisten each end and shape the roll into a circle, sealing the ends together. With sharp scissors, make little cuts around the top for decoration. Place on a greased baking (cookie) sheet and brush with the remaining egg. Leave to rest for 15 minutes.

Bake in a preheated oven at 230°C/450°F/gas mark 8 for 25 minutes until golden brown. Brush with honey and leave to cool.

Banana Loaf

Makes one 900 g/2 lb loaf

75 g/3 oz/1/3 cup butter or margarine, softened

175 g/6 oz/2/3 cup caster (superfine) sugar

2 eggs, lightly beaten

450 g/1 lb ripe bananas, mashed

200 g/7 oz/1¾ cup self-raising (self-rising) flour

75 g/3 oz/¾ cup walnuts, chopped

100 g/4 oz/2/3 cup sultanas (golden raisins)

50 g/2 oz/½ cup glacé (candied) cherries

2.5 ml/½ tsp bicarbonate of soda (baking soda)

A pinch of salt

Cream together the butter or margarine and sugar until pale and fluffy. Gradually beat in the eggs, then stir in the bananas. Mix in the remaining ingredients until well blended. Spoon into a greased and lined 900 g/2 lb loaf tin (pan) and bake in a preheated oven at 180°C/350°C/gas mark 4 for 1¼ hours until well risen and firm to the touch.

Wholemeal Banana Bread

Makes one 900 g/2 lb loaf

100 g/4 oz/½ cup butter or margarine, softened

50 g/2 oz/¼ cup soft brown sugar

2 eggs, lightly beaten

3 bananas, mashed

175 g/6 oz/1½ cups wholemeal (wholewheat) flour

100 g/4 oz/1 cup oat flour

5 ml/1 tsp baking powder

5 ml/1 tsp ground mixed (apple-pie) spice

30 ml/2 tbsp milk

Cream together the butter or margarine and sugar until light and fluffy. Gradually beat in the eggs, stir in the bananas, then fold in the flours, baking powder and mixed spice. Add enough of the milk to make a soft mixture. Spoon into a greased and lined 900 g/2 lb loaf tin (pan) and level the surface. Bake in a preheated oven at 190°C/375°F/gas mark 5 until risen and golden brown.

Banana and Nut Bread

Makes one 900 g/2 lb loaf

50 g/2 oz/¼ cup butter or margarine

225 g/8 oz/2 cups self-raising (self-rising) flour

50 g/2 oz/¼ cup caster (superfine) sugar

50 g/2 oz/½ cup chopped mixed nuts

1 egg, lightly beaten

75 g/3 oz/1/3 cup golden (light corn) syrup

2 bananas, mashed

15 ml/1 tbsp milk

Rub the butter or margarine into the flour, then stir in the sugar and nuts. Mix in the egg, syrup and bananas and enough of the milk to give a soft mixture. Spoon into a greased and lined 900 g/2 lb loaf tin (pan) and bake in a preheated oven at 180°C/350°F/gas mark 4 for about 1 hour until firm and golden brown. Store for 24 hours before serving sliced and buttered.

Bara Brith

Makes three 450 g/1 lb loaves

450 g/1 lb/2¾ cups dried mixed fruit (fruit cake mix)

250 ml/8 fl oz/1 cup strong cold tea

30 ml/2 tbsp dried yeast

175 g/6 oz/¾ cup soft brown sugar

250 g/12 oz/3 cups wholemeal (wholewheat) flour

350 g/12 oz/3 cups strong plain (bread) flour

10 ml/2 tsp ground mixed (apple-pie) spice

100 g/4 oz/½ cup butter or margarine, melted

2 eggs, beaten

2.5 ml/½ tsp salt

15 ml/1 tbsp clear honey

Soak the fruit in the tea for 2 hours. Warm 30 ml/2 tbsp of the tea and mix with the yeast and 5 ml/1 tsp of the sugar. Leave in a warm place until frothy. Mix together the dry ingredients, then blend in the yeast mixture and all remaining ingredients except the honey and mix to a dough. Turn out on to a lightly floured surface and knead gently until smooth and elastic. Divide between three greased and lined 450 g/1 lb loaf tins (pans). Cover with oiled clingfilm (plastic wrap) and leave in a warm place for 1 hour until the dough has risen above the top of the tins.

Bake in a preheated oven at 200°C/400°F/gas mark 6 for 15 minutes, then reduce the oven temperature to 180°C/350°F/gas mark 4 for a further 45 minutes until golden and hollow-sounding when tapped on the base. Warm the honey and brush over the tops of the warm loaves.

Bath Buns

Makes 12 buns

500 g/1 lb/4 cups strong plain (bread) flour

25 g/1 oz fresh yeast or 40 ml/2½ tbsp dried yeast

150 ml/¼ pt/2/3 cup warm milk

75 g/3 oz/1/3 cup caster (superfine) sugar

150 ml/¼ pt/2/3 cup warm water

5 ml/1 tsp salt

50 g/2 oz/¼ cup butter or margarine

2 eggs, beaten

175 g/6 oz/1 cup sultanas (golden raisins)

50 g/2 oz/1/3 cup chopped mixed peel

Beaten egg for glazing

Preserving sugar, crushed, for sprinkling

Place a quarter of the flour in a bowl and make a well in the centre. Mix the yeast with half the milk and 5 ml/1 tsp of the sugar and pour into the well. Add the remaining liquid. Stir together and leave in a warm place for 35 minutes until frothy. Place the remaining flour in a bowl with the salt. Stir in the remaining sugar, then rub in the butter or margarine until the mixture resembles breadcrumbs. Pour in the yeast mixture and eggs and beat well. Stir in the sultanas and mixed peel. Cover with oiled clingfilm (plastic wrap) and leave in a warm place until doubled in size.

Knead the dough well and divide into 12 pieces. Shape into a round and place on a greased baking (cookie) sheet. Cover with oiled clingfilm and leave in a warm place for 15 minutes. Brush with beaten egg and sprinkle with crushed sugar. Bake in a preheated oven at 200°C/400°F/gas mark 6 for 15–20 minutes until golden.

Cherry and Honey Loaf

Makes one 900 g/2 lb loaf

175 g/6 oz/¾ cup butter or margarine, softened

75 g/3 oz/1/3 cup soft brown sugar

60 ml/4 tbsp clear honey

2 eggs, beaten

100 g/4 oz/2 cups wholemeal (wholewheat) flour

10 ml/2 tsp baking powder

100 g/4 oz/½ cup glacé (candied) cherries, chopped

45 ml/3 tbsp milk

Cream together the butter or margarine, sugar and honey until light and fluffy. Gradually stir in the eggs, beating well after each addition. Mix in the remaining ingredients to make a soft mixture. Spoon into a greased and lined 900 g/2 lb loaf tin (pan) and bake in a preheated oven at 180°C/350°F/gas mark 4 for 1 hour until a skewer inserted in the centre comes out clean. Serve sliced and buttered.

Cinnamon and Nutmeg Rolls

Makes 24

15 ml/1 tbsp dried yeast

120 ml/4 fl oz/½ cup milk, boiled

50 g/2 oz/¼ cup caster (superfine) sugar

50 g/2 oz/¼ cup lard (shortening)

5 ml/1 tsp salt

120 ml/4 fl oz/½ cup warm water

2.5 ml/½ tsp grated nutmeg

1 egg, beaten

400 g/14 oz/3½ cups strong plain (bread) flour

45 ml/3 tbsp butter or margarine, melted

175 g/6 oz/¾ cup soft brown sugar

10 ml/2 tsp ground cinnamon

75 g/3 oz/½ cup raisins

Dissolve the yeast in the warm milk with a teaspoon of the caster sugar and leave until frothy. Mix together the remaining caster sugar, the lard and salt. Pour in the water and stir until blended. Stir in the yeast mixture, then gradually add the nutmeg, egg and flour. Knead to a smooth dough. Place in a greased bowl, cover with oiled clingfilm (plastic wrap) and leave in a warm place for about 1 hour until doubled in size.

Divide the dough in half and roll out on a lightly floured surface into rectangles about 5 mm/¼ in thick. Brush with melted butter and sprinkle with the brown sugar, cinnamon and raisins. Roll up from the longer size and cut each roll into 12 slices 1 cm/½ in thick. Place the slices a little way apart on a greased baking (cookie) sheet and leave in a warm place for 1 hour. Bake in a preheated oven at 190°C/375°F/gas mark 5 for 20 minutes until well risen.

Cranberry Bread

Makes one 450 g/1 lb loaf

225 g/8 oz/2 cups plain (all-purpose) flour

2.5 ml/½ tsp salt

2.5 ml/½ tsp bicarbonate of soda (baking soda)

225 g/8 oz/1 cup caster (superfine) sugar

7.5 ml/1½ tsp baking powder

Juice and grated rind of 1 orange

1 egg, beaten

25 g/1 oz/2 tbsp lard (shortening), melted

100 g/4 oz fresh or frozen cranberries, crushed

50 g/2 oz/½ cup walnuts, coarsely chopped

Mix together the dry ingredients in a large bowl. Put the orange juice and rind in a measuring jug and make up to 175 ml/6 fl oz/¾ cup with water. Stir into the dry ingredients with the egg and lard. Stir in the cranberries and nuts. Spoon into a greased 450 g/1 lb loaf tin (pan) and bake in a preheated oven at 160°C/325°F/gas mark 3 for about 1 hour until a skewer inserted in the centre comes out clean. Leave to cool, then keep for 24 hours before cutting.

Date and Butter Loaf

Makes one 900 g/2 lb loaf

For the loaf:

175 g/6 oz/1 cup stoned (pitted) dates, finely chopped

5 ml/1 tsp bicarbonate of soda (baking soda)

250 ml/8 fl oz/1 cup boiling water

75 g/3 oz/1/3 cup butter or margarine, softened

225 g/8 oz/1 cup soft brown sugar

1 egg, lightly beaten

5 ml/1 tsp vanilla essence (extract)

225 g/8 oz/2 cups plain (all-purpose) flour

5 ml/1 tsp baking powder

A pinch of salt

For the topping:

100 g/4 oz/½ cup soft brown sugar

50 g/2 oz/¼ cup butter or margarine

120 ml/4 fl oz/½ cup single (light) cream

To make the loaf, mix together the dates, bicarbonate of soda and boiling water and stir well, then leave to cool. Cream together the butter or margarine and sugar until light and fluffy, then gradually beat in the egg and vanilla essence. Stir in the flour, baking powder and salt. Spoon the mixture into a greased and lined 900 g/2 lb loaf tin (pan) and bake in a preheated oven at 180°C/350°F/gas mark 4 for 1 hour until a skewer inserted in the centre comes out clean.

To make the topping, melt together the sugar, butter or margarine and cream over a low heat until blended, then simmer very gently for 15 minutes, stirring occasionally. Remove the loaf from the tin and pour over the hot topping. Leave to cool.

Date and Banana Bread

Makes one 900 g/2 lb loaf

225 g/8 oz/1 1/3 cups stoned (pitted) dates, chopped

300 ml/½ pt/1¼ cups milk

5 ml/1 tsp bicarbonate of soda (baking soda)

100 g/4 oz/½ cup butter or margarine

275 g/10 oz/2½ cups self-raising (self-rising) flour

2 ripe bananas, mashed

1 egg, beaten

75 g/3 oz/¾ cup hazelnuts, chopped

30 ml/2 tbsp clear honey

Place the dates, milk and bicarbonate of soda in a pan and bring to the boil, stirring. Leave to cool. Rub the butter or margarine into the flour until the mixture resembles breadcrumbs. Stir in the bananas, egg and most of the hazelnuts, reserving a few for decoration. Spoon into a greased and lined 900 g/2 lb loaf tin (pan) and bake in a preheated oven at 180°C/350°F/gas mark 4 for 1 hour until a skewer inserted in the centre comes out clean. Leave to cool in the tin for 5 minutes, then turn out and remove the lining paper. Warm the honey and brush over the top of the cake. Sprinkle with the reserved nuts and leave to cool completely.

Date and Orange Loaf

Makes one 900 g/2 lb loaf

225 g/8 oz/1 1/3 cups stoned (pitted) dates, chopped

120 ml/4 fl oz/½ cup water

200 g/7 oz/scant 1 cup soft brown sugar

75 g/3 oz/1/3 cup butter or margarine

Grated rind and juice of 1 orange

1 egg, lightly beaten

225 g/8 oz/2 cups plain (all-purpose) flour

10 ml/2 tsp baking powder

5 ml/1 tsp ground cinnamon

Simmer the dates in the water for 15 minutes until pulpy. Stir in the sugar until dissolved. Remove from the heat and leave to cool slightly. Beat in the butter or margarine, orange rind and juice, then the egg. Beat in the flour, baking powder and cinnamon. Spoon into a greased and lined 900 g/2 lb loaf tin (pan) and bake in a preheated oven at 180°C/350°F/gas mark 4 for 1 hour until a skewer inserted in the centre comes out clean.

Date and Nut Bread

Makes one 900 g/2 lb loaf

250 ml/8 fl oz/1 cup boiling water

225 g/8 oz/1 1/3 cups stoned (pitted) dates, chopped

10 ml/2 tsp bicarbonate of soda (baking soda)

25 g/1 oz/2 tbsp vegetable fat (shortening)

225 g/8 oz/1 cup soft brown sugar

2 eggs, beaten

225 g/8 oz/2 cups plain (all-purpose) flour

5 ml/1 tsp salt

50 g/2 oz/½ cup pecan nuts, chopped

Pour the boiling water over the dates and bicarbonate of soda and leave until lukewarm. Cream together the vegetable fat and sugar until creamy. Gradually beat in the eggs. Mix the flour with the salt and nuts, then fold into the creamed mixture alternately with the dates and liquid. Spoon into a greased 900 g/2 lb loaf tin (pan) and bake in a preheated oven at 180°C/350°F/gas mark 4 for 1 hour until firm to the touch.

Date Tea Bread

Makes one 900 g/2 lb loaf

225 g/8 oz/2 cups plain (all-purpose) flour

100 g/4 oz/½ cup soft brown sugar

A pinch of salt

5 ml/1 tsp ground mixed (apple-pie) spice

5 ml/1 tsp bicarbonate of soda (baking soda)

50 g/2 oz/¼ cup butter or margarine, melted

15 ml/1 tbsp black treacle (molasses)

150 ml/¼ pt/2/3 cup black tea

1 egg, beaten

75 g/3 oz/½ cup stoned (pitted) dates, chopped

Mix together the flour, sugar, salt, spice and bicarbonate of soda. Stir in the butter, treacle, tea and egg and mix well until smooth. Stir in the dates. Spoon the mixture into a greased and lined 900 g/2 lb loaf tin (pan) and bake in a preheated oven at 180°C/350°F/gas mark 4 for 45 minutes.

Date and Walnut Loaf

Makes one 900 g/2 lb loaf

100 g/4 oz/½ cup butter or margarine

175 g/6 oz/1½ cups wholemeal (wholewheat) flour

50 g/2 oz/½ cup oat flour

10 ml/2 tsp baking powder

5 ml/1 tsp ground mixed (apple-pie) spice

2.5 ml/½ tsp ground cinnamon

50 g/2 oz/¼ cup soft brown sugar

75 g/3 oz/½ cup stoned (pitted) dates, chopped

75 g/3 oz/¾ cup walnuts, chopped

2 eggs, lightly beaten

30 ml/2 tbsp milk

Rub the butter or margarine into the flours, baking powder and spices until the mixture resembles breadcrumbs. Stir in the sugar, dates and walnuts. Mix in the eggs and milk to make a soft dough. Shape the dough into a greased 900 g/2 lb loaf tin (pan) and level the top. Bake in a preheated oven at 160°C/325°F/gas mark 3 for 45 minutes until risen and golden .

Fig Loaf

Makes one 450 g/1 lb loaf

100 g/4 oz/1½ cups bran cereal

100 g/4 oz/½ cup soft brown sugar

100 g/4 oz/2/3 cup dried figs, chopped

30 ml/2 tbsp black treacle (molasses)

250 ml/8 fl oz/1 cup milk

100 g/4 oz/1 cup wholemeal (wholewheat) flour

10 ml/2 tsp baking powder

Mix the cereal, sugar, figs, treacle and milk and leave to stand for 30 minutes. Stir in the flour and baking powder. Spoon into a greased 450 g/1 lb loaf tin (pan) and bake in a preheated oven at 180°C/350°F/gas mark 4 for 45 minutes until firm and a skewer inserted in the centre comes out clean.

Fig and Marsala Bread

Makes one 900 g/2 lb loaf

225 g/8 oz/1 cup unsalted (sweet) butter or margarine, softened

225 g/8 oz/1 cup soft brown sugar

4 eggs, lightly beaten

45 ml/3 tbsp Marsala

5 ml/1 tsp vanilla essence (extract)

200 g/7 oz/1¾ cups plain (all-purpose) flour

A pinch of salt

50 g/2 oz/1/3 cup ready-to-eat dried apricots, chopped

50 g/2 oz/1/3 cup stoned (pitted) dates, chopped

50 g/2 oz/1/3 cup dried figs, chopped

50 g/2 oz/½ cup chopped mixed nuts

Cream together the butter or margarine and sugar until light and fluffy. Gradually add the eggs, then the Marsala and vanilla essence. Mix the flour and salt with the fruit and nuts, then fold into the mixture and mix well. Spoon into a greased and floured 900 g/2 lb loaf tin (pan) and bake in a preheated oven at 180°C/350°F/gas mark 4 for 1 hour. Leave to cool in the tin for 10 minutes, then turn out on to a wire rack to finish cooling.

Honey and Fig Rolls

Makes 12

25 g/1 oz fresh yeast or 40 ml/2½ tbsp dried yeast

75 g/3 oz/¼ cup clear honey

300 ml/½ pt/1¼ cups warm water

100 g/4 oz/2/3 cup dried figs, chopped

15 ml/1 tbsp malt extract

450 g/1 lb/4 cups wholemeal (wholewheat) flour

15 ml/1 tbsp milk powder (non-fat dry milk)

5 ml/1 tsp salt

2.5 ml/½ tsp grated nutmeg

40 g/1½ oz/2½ tbsp butter or margarine

Grated zest of 1 orange

1 egg, beaten

15 ml/1 tbsp sesame seeds

Blend the yeast with 5 ml/1 tsp of the honey and a little of the warm water and leave in a warm place until frothy. Mix the remaining warm water with the figs, malt extract and remaining honey and leave to soak. Mix together the flour, milk powder, salt and nutmeg, then rub in the butter or margarine and stir in the orange rind. Make a well in the centre and pour in the yeast mixture and the fig mixture. Mix to a soft dough and knead until no longer sticky. Place in an oiled bowl, cover with oiled clingfilm (plastic wrap) and leave in a warm place for 1 hour until doubled in size.

Knead lightly, then shape into 12 rolls and arrange on a greased baking (cookie) sheet. Cover with oiled clingfilm and leave in a warm place for 20 minutes. Brush with beaten egg and sprinkle with sesame seeds. Bake in a preheated oven at 230°C/450°F/gas mark 8 for 15 minutes until golden brown and hollow-sounding when tapped on the base.

Hot Cross Buns

Makes 12

For the buns:

450 g/1 lb/4 cups strong (bread) flour

15 ml/1 tbsp dried yeast

A pinch of salt

5 ml/1 tsp ground mixed (apple-pie) spice

50 g/2 oz/¼ cup caster (superfine) sugar

100 g/4 oz/2/3 cup currants

25 g/1 oz/3 tbsp chopped mixed (candied) peel

1 egg, beaten

250 ml/8 fl oz/1 cup milk

50 g/2 oz/¼ cup butter or margarine, melted

For the crosses:

25 g/1 oz/¼ cup plain (all-purpose) flour

15 ml/1 tbsp water

A little beaten egg

For the glaze:

50 g/2 oz/¼ cup caster (superfine) sugar

150 ml/¼ pt/2/3 cup water

To make the buns, mix together the dry ingredients, currants and mixed peel. Stir in the egg, milk and melted butter and mix to a firm dough that comes away from the sides of the bowl. Turn out on to a lightly floured surface and knead for 5 minutes until smooth and elastic. Divide into 12 and roll into balls. Place well apart on a greased baking (cookie) sheet, cover with oiled clingfilm (plastic wrap) and leave in a warm place for about 45 minutes until doubled in size.

Put the flour for the cross in a small bowl and gradually mix in enough of the water to make a dough. Roll out to a long strand. Brush the tops of the buns with beaten egg, then gently press a cross of dough cut from the long strand into each one. Bake in a preheated oven at 220°C/425°F/gas mark 7 for 20 minutes until golden brown.

To make the glaze, dissolve the sugar in the water, then boil until syrupy. Brush over the hot buns, then transfer them to a wire rack to cool.

Lincolnshire Plum Bread

Makes three 450 g/1 lb loaves

15 g/½ oz fresh yeast or 20 ml/4 tsp dried yeast

45 ml/3 tbsp soft brown sugar

200 ml/7 fl oz/scant 1 cup warm milk

100 g/4 oz/½ cup butter or margarine

450 g/1 lb/4 cups plain (all-purpose) flour

10 ml/2 tsp baking powder

A pinch of salt

1 egg, beaten

450 g/1 lb/22/3 cups dried mixed fruit (fruit cake mix)

Blend the yeast with 5 ml/1 tsp of the sugar and a little of the warm milk and leave in a warm place for 20 minutes until frothy. Rub the butter or margarine into the flour, baking powder and salt until the mixture resembles breadcrumbs. Stir in the remaining sugar and make a well in the centre. Mix in the yeast mixture, remaining warm milk and the egg, then work in the fruit to make a fairly stiff dough. Shape into three greased 450 g/1 lb loaf tins (pans) and bake in a preheated oven at 150°C/300°F/gas mark 2 for 2 hours until golden brown.

London Buns

Makes 10

50 g/2 oz fresh yeast or 30 ml/2 tbsp dried yeast

75 g/3 oz/1/3 cup soft brown sugar

300 ml/½ pt/1¼ cups warm water

175 g/6 oz/1 cup currants

25 g/1 oz/3 tbsp chopped stoned (pitted) dates

25 g/1 oz/3 tbsp chopped mixed (candied) peel

25 g/1 oz/2 tbsp chopped glacé (candied) cherries

45 ml/3 tbsp orange juice

450 g/1 lb/4 cups wholemeal (wholewheat) flour

2.5 ml/½ tsp salt

25 g/1 oz/¼ cup milk powder (non-fat dry milk)

15 ml/1 tbsp ground mixed (apple-pie) spice

5 ml/1 tsp ground cinnamon

75 g/3 oz/1/3 cup butter or margarine

15 ml/1 tbsp grated orange rind

1 egg

15 ml/1 tbsp clear honey

30 ml/2 tbsp flaked (slivered) almonds

Blend the yeast with a little of the sugar and a little of the warm water and leave in a warm place for 20 minutes until frothy. Soak the currants, dates, mixed peel and cherries in the orange juice. Mix together the flour, salt, milk powder and spices. Rub in the butter or margarine, then stir in the orange rind and make a well in the centre. Add the yeast mixture, the remaining warm water and the egg and mix to a smooth dough. Place in an oiled bowl, cover with clingfilm (plastic wrap) and leave in a warm place for 1 hour until doubled in size.

Shape the dough into 10 rolls and arrange on a greased baking (cookie) sheet. Cover with oiled clingfilm and leave in a warm place for 45 minutes. Bake in a preheated oven at 230°C/450°F/gas mark 8 for 15 minutes until well risen. Brush with the honey, sprinkle with the almonds and leave to cool.

Irish Country Loaf

Makes one 900 g/2 lb loaf

350 g/12 oz/3 cups wholemeal (wholewheat) flour

100 g/4 oz/1 cup oatmeal

100 g/4 oz/2/3 cup sultanas (golden raisins)

15 ml/1 tbsp baking powder

15 ml/1 tbsp caster (superfine) sugar

5 ml/1 tsp bicarbonate of soda (baking soda)

5 ml/1 tsp salt

10 ml/2 tsp ground mixed (apple-pie) spice

Grated rind of ½ lemon

1 egg, beaten

300 ml/½ pt/1¼ cups buttermilk or plain yoghurt

150 ml/¼ pt/2/3 cup water

Mix together all the dry ingredients and lemon rind and make a well in the centre. Beat together the egg, buttermilk or yoghurt and water. Mix into the dry ingredients and work to a soft dough. Knead on a lightly floured surface, then shape into a greased 900 g/2 lb loaf tin (pan). Bake in a preheated oven at 200°C/400°F/gas mark 6 for 1 hour until well risen and firm to the touch.

Malt Loaf

Makes one 450 g/1 lb loaf

25 g/1 oz/2 tbsp butter or margarine

225 g/8 oz/2 cups self-raising (self-rising) flour

25 g/1 oz/2 tbsp soft brown sugar

30 ml/2 tbsp black treacle (molasses)

20 ml/4 tsp malt extract

150 ml/¼ pt/2/3 cup milk

75 g/3 oz/½ cup sultanas (golden raisins)

15 ml/1 tbsp caster (superfine) sugar

30 ml/2 tbsp water

Rub the butter or margarine into the flour, then stir in the brown sugar. Warm the treacle, malt extract and milk, then blend into the dry ingredients with the sultanas and mix to a dough. Turn into a greased 450 g/1 lb loaf tin (pan) and bake in a preheated oven at 160°C/325°F/gas mark 3 for 1 hour until golden. Bring the sugar and water to the boil and boil until syrupy. Brush over the top of the loaf and leave to cool.

Bran Malt Loaf

Makes one 450 g/1 lb loaf

100 g/4 oz/½ cup soft brown sugar

225 g/8 oz/1 1/3 cups dried mixed fruit (fruit cake mix)

75 g/3 oz All Bran cereal

250 ml/8 fl oz/1 cup milk

5 ml/1 tsp ground mixed (apple-pie) spice

100 g/4 oz/1 cup self-raising (self-rising) flour

Mix together the sugar, fruit, All Bran, milk and spice and leave to soak for 1 hour. Stir in the flour and mix well. Spoon into a greased and lined 450 g/1 lb loaf tin (pan) and bake in a preheated oven at 180°C/350°F/gas mark 4 for 1½ hours until firm to the touch.

Wholemeal Malt Loaf

Makes one 900 g/2 lb loaf

25 g/1 oz/2 tbsp butter or margarine

30 ml/2 tbsp black treacle (molasses)

45 ml/3 tbsp malt extract

150 ml/¼ pt/2/3 cup milk

175 g/6 oz/1½ cups wholemeal (wholewheat) flour

75 g/3 oz/¾ cup oat flour

10 ml/2 tsp baking powder

100 g/4 oz/2/3 cup raisins

Melt the butter or margarine, treacle, malt extract and milk. Pour into the flours, baking powder and raisins and mix to a soft dough. Spoon into a greased 900 g/2 lb loaf tin (pan) and level the surface. Bake in a preheated oven at 200°C/400°F/gas mark 6 for 45 minutes until a skewer inserted in the centre comes out clean.

Freda's Nut Loaf

Makes three 350 g/12 oz loaves

25 g/1 oz fresh yeast or 40 ml/2½ tbsp dried yeast

10 ml/2 tsp malt extract

375 ml/13 fl oz/1½ cups warm water

450 g/1 lb/4 cups wholemeal (wholewheat) flour

5 ml/1 tsp soya flour

50 g/2 oz/½ cup rolled oats

2.5 ml/½ tsp salt

25 g/1 oz/2 tbsp soft brown sugar

15 ml/1 tbsp lard (shortening)

100 g/4 oz/1 cup chopped mixed nuts

175 g/6 oz/1 cup currants

50 g/2 oz/1/3 cup stoned (pitted) dates, chopped

50 g/2 oz/1/3 cup raisins

2.5 ml/½ tsp ground cinnamon

1 egg, beaten

45 ml/3 tbsp flaked (slivered) almonds

Blend the yeast with the malt extract and a little of the warm water and leave in a warm place until frothy. Mix together the flours, oats, salt and sugar, rub in the lard and make a well in the centre. Mix in the yeast mixture and the remaining warm water and knead to a smooth dough. Mix in the nuts, currants, dates, raisins and cinnamon. Knead until elastic and no longer sticky. Place the dough in an oiled bowl and cover with oiled clingfilm (plastic wrap). Leave in a warm place for 1 hour until doubled in size.

Knead the dough lightly, then shape into three rounds and flatten slightly, then place on a greased baking (cookie) sheet. Brush the tops with beaten egg and sprinkle with the almonds. Bake in a preheated oven at 230°C/450°F/gas mark 8 for 35 minutes until well risen and hollow-sounding when tapped on the base.

Brazil Nut and Date Loaf

Makes three 350 g/12 oz loaves

25 g/1 oz fresh yeast or 40 ml/2½ tbsp dried yeast

10 ml/2 tsp malt extract

375 ml/13 fl oz/1½ cups warm water

450 g/1 lb/4 cups wholemeal (wholewheat) flour

5 ml/1 tsp soya flour

50 g/2 oz/½ cup rolled oats

2.5 ml/½ tsp salt

25 g/1 oz/2 tbsp soft brown sugar

15 ml/1 tbsp lard (shortening)

100 g/4 oz/1 cup brazil nuts, chopped

250 g/9 oz/1½ cup stoned (pitted) dates, chopped

2.5 ml/½ tsp ground cinnamon

1 egg, beaten

45 ml/3 tbsp sliced brazil nuts

Blend the yeast with the malt extract and a little of the warm water and leave in a warm place until frothy. Mix together the flours, oats, salt and sugar, rub in the lard and make a well in the centre. Mix in the yeast mixture and the remaining warm water and knead to a smooth dough. Mix in the nuts, dates and cinnamon. Knead until elastic and no longer sticky. Place the dough in an oiled bowl and cover with oiled clingfilm (plastic wrap). Leave in a warm place for 1 hour until doubled in size.

Knead the dough lightly, shape into three rounds and flatten slightly, then place on a greased baking (cookie) sheet. Brush the tops with beaten egg and sprinkle with the sliced brazil nuts. Bake in a preheated oven at 230°C/450°F/gas mark 8 for 35 minutes until well risen and hollow-sounding when tapped on the base.

Panastan Fruit Bread

Makes three 175 g/12 oz loaves

25 g/1 oz fresh yeast or 40 ml/2½ tbsp dried yeast

150 ml/¼ pt/2/3 cup warm water

60 ml/4 tbsp clear honey

5 ml/1 tsp malt extract

15 ml/1 tbsp sunflower seeds

15 ml/1 tbsp sesame seeds

25 g/1 oz/¼ cup wheatgerm

450 g/1 lb/4 cups wholemeal (wholewheat) flour

5 ml/1 tsp salt

50 g/2 oz/¼ cup butter or margarine

175 g/6 oz/1 cup sultanas (golden raisins)

25 g/1 oz/3 tbsp chopped mixed (candied) peel

1 egg, beaten

Blend the yeast with a little of the warm water and 5 ml/1 tsp of the honey and leave in a warm place for 20 minutes until frothy. Mix the remaining honey and the malt extract into the remaining warm water. Toast the sunflower and sesame seeds and the wheatgerm in a dry pan, shaking until golden brown. Place in a bowl with the flour and salt and rub in the butter or margarine. Stir in the sultanas and mixed peel and make a well in the centre. Add the yeast mixture, the water mixture and the egg and knead to a smooth dough. Place in an oiled bowl, cover with oiled clingfilm (plastic wrap) and leave in a warm place for 1 hour until doubled in size.

Knead lightly, then shape into three loaves and place on a greased baking (cookie) sheet or in greased baking tins (pans). Cover with oiled clingfilm and leave in a warm place for 20 minutes. Bake in a preheated oven at 230°C/450°F/gas mark 8 for 40 minutes until golden brown and hollow-sounding when tapped on the base.

Pumpkin Loaf

Makes two 450 g/1 lb loaves

350 g/12 oz/1½ cups caster (superfine) sugar

120 ml/4 fl oz/½ cup oil

2.5 ml/½ tsp grated nutmeg

5 ml/1 tsp ground cinnamon

5 ml/1 tsp salt

2 eggs, beaten

225 g/8 oz/1 cup cooked, mashed pumpkin

60 ml/4 tbsp water

2.5 ml/½ tsp bicarbonate of soda (baking soda)

1.5 ml/¼ tsp baking powder

175 g/6 oz/1½ cups plain (all-purpose) flour

Mix together the sugar, oil, nutmeg, cinnamon, salt and eggs and beat well. Stir in the remaining ingredients and mix to a smooth batter. Pour into two greased 450 g/1 lb loaf tins (pans) and bake in a preheated oven at 180°C/350°F/gas mark 4 for 1 hour until a skewer inserted in the centre comes out clean.

Raisin Bread

Makes two 450 g/1 lb loaves

15 ml/1 tbsp dried yeast

120 ml/4 fl oz/½ cup warm water

250 ml/8 fl oz/1 cup warm milk

60 ml/4 tbsp oil

50 g/2 oz/¼ cup sugar

1 egg, beaten

10 ml/2 tsp ground cinnamon

5 ml/1 tsp salt

225 g/8 oz/1 1/3 cups raisins, soaked in cold water overnight

550 g/1¼ lb/5 cups strong plain (bread) flour

Dissolve the yeast in the warm water and leave until frothy. Mix together the milk, oil, sugar, egg, cinnamon and salt. Drain the raisins and stir them into the mixture. Stir in the yeast mixture. Gradually work in the flour and mix to a stiff dough. Place in a greased bowl and cover with oiled clingfilm (plastic wrap). Leave in a warm place for about 1 hour to rise until doubled in size.

Knead again and shape into two greased 450 g/1 lb loaf tins (pans). Cover with oiled clingfilm and leave in a warm place again until the dough rises above the top of the tins. Bake in a preheated oven at 150°C/300°F/gas mark 2 for 1 hour until golden.

Raisin Soak

Makes two 450 g/l lb loaves

450 g/1 lb/4 cups plain (all-purpose) flour

2.5 ml/½ tsp salt

5 ml/1 tsp ground mixed (apple-pie) spice

225 g/8 oz/11/3 cups raisins, chopped

10 ml/2 tsp bicarbonate of soda (baking soda)

100 g/4 oz/½ cup butter or margarine, melted

225 g/8 oz/1 cup caster (superfine) sugar

450 ml/¾ pt/2 cups milk

15 ml/1 tbsp lemon juice

30 ml/2 tbsp apricot jam (conserve), sieved (strained)

Mix together the flour, salt, mixed spice and raisins. Stir the bicarbonate of soda into the melted butter until blended, then stir all the ingredients together until well mixed. Cover and leave to stand overnight.

Spoon the mixture into two greased and lined 450 g/1 lb loaf tins (pans) and bake in a preheated oven at 180°C/350°F/gas mark 4 for 1 hour until a skewer inserted in the centre comes out clean.

Rhubarb and Date Bread

Makes one 900 g/2 lb loaf

225 g/8 oz rhubarb, chopped

50 g/2 oz/¼ cup butter or margarine

225 g/8 oz/2 cups plain (all-purpose) flour

15 ml/1 tbsp baking powder

175 g/6 oz/1 cup dates, stoned (pitted) and finely chopped

1 egg, beaten

60 ml/4 tbsp milk

Wash the rhubarb and cook gently in just the water clinging to the pieces until you have a purée. Rub the butter or margarine into the flour and baking powder until the mixture resembles breadcrumbs. Stir in the rhubarb, dates, egg and milk and blend together well. Spoon into a greased and lined 900 g/2 lb loaf tin (pan) and bake in a preheated oven at 190°C/375°F/gas mark 5 for 1 hour until firm to the touch.

Rice Bread

Makes one 900 g/2 lb loaf

75 g/3 oz/1/3 cup arborio or other medium-grain rice

500 ml/17 fl oz/2½ cups lukewarm water

15 g/½ oz fresh yeast or 20 ml/4 tsp dried yeast

30 ml/2 tbsp warm water

550 g/1¼ lb/6 cups strong plain (bread) flour

15 ml/1 tbsp salt

Put the rice and half the lukewarm water in a pan, bring to the boil, cover, and simmer very gently for about 25 minutes until the rice has absorbed all the liquid and bubble holes appear on the surface.

Meanwhile, mix the yeast with the warm water. When the rice is cooked, stir in the flour, salt, yeast mixture and the remaining lukewarm water and mix to a wet dough. Cover with oiled clingfilm (plastic wrap) and leave in a warm place for about 1 hour until doubled in size.

Knead the dough on a floured surface, then shape into a greased 900 g/2 lb loaf tin (pan). Cover with oiled clingfilm and leave in a warm place until the dough rises above the top of the tin. Bake in a preheated oven at 230°C/450°F/gas mark 8 for 15 minutes, then reduce the oven temperature to 200°C/400°F/gas mark 6 and bake for a further 15 minutes. Turn out of the tin and return to the oven for a further 15 minutes until crisp and brown.

Rice and Nut Tea Bread

Makes two 900 g/2 lb loaves

100 g/4 oz/½ cup long-grain rice

300 ml/½ pt/1¼ cups orange juice

400 g/14 oz/1¾ cups caster (superfine) sugar

2 eggs, beaten

50 g/2 oz/¼ cup butter or margarine, melted

Grated rind and juice of 1 orange

225 g/8 oz/2 cups plain (all-purpose) flour

175 g/6 oz/1½ cups wholemeal (wholewheat) flour

10 ml/2 tsp baking powder

5 ml/1 tsp bicarbonate of soda (baking soda)

5 ml/1 tsp salt

50 g/2 oz/½ cup walnuts, chopped

50 g/2 oz/1/3 cup sultanas (golden raisins)

50 g/2 oz/1/3 cup icing (confectioners') sugar, sifted

Cook the rice in plenty of boiling salted water for about 15 minutes until tender, then drain, rinse in cold water and drain again. Mix together the orange juice, sugar, eggs, melted butter or margarine and all but 2.5 ml/½ tsp of the orange rind – reserve the rest and the juice for the icing (frosting). Mix together the flours, baking powder, bicarbonate of soda and salt and fold in to the sugar mixture. Fold in the rice, nuts and sultanas. Spoon the mixture into two greased 900 g/2 lb loaf tins (pans) and bake in a preheated oven at 180°C/350°F/gas mark 4 for 1 hour until a skewer inserted in the centre comes out clean. Leave to cool in the tins for 10 minutes, then turn out on to a wire rack to finish cooling.

Blend the icing sugar with the reserved orange rind and enough of the juice to make a smooth, thick paste. Drizzle over the loaves and leave to set. Serve sliced and buttered.

Curly Sugar Rolls

Makes about 10

50 g/2 oz fresh yeast or 75 ml/5 tbsp dried yeast

75 g/3 oz/1/3 cup soft brown sugar

300 ml/½ pt/1¼ cups warm water

175 g/6 oz/1 cup currants

25 g/1 oz/3 tbsp stoned (pitted) dates, chopped

45 ml/3 tbsp orange juice

450 g/1 lb/4 cups wholemeal (wholewheat) flour

2.5 ml/½ tsp salt

25 g/1 oz/¼ cup milk powder (non-fat dry milk)

15 ml/1 tbsp ground mixed (apple-pie) spice

75 g/3 oz/1/3 cup butter or margarine

15 ml/1 tbsp grated orange rind

1 egg

For the filling:

30 ml/2 tbsp oil

75 g/3 oz/1/3 cup demerara sugar

For the glaze:

15 ml/1 tbsp clear honey

30 ml/2 tbsp chopped walnuts

Blend the yeast with a little of the soft brown sugar and a little of the warm water and leave in a warm place for 20 minutes until frothy. Soak the currants and dates in the orange juice. Mix together the flour, salt, milk powder and mixed spice. Rub in the butter or margarine, then stir in the orange rind and make a well in the centre. Add the yeast mixture, the remaining warm water and the egg and mix to a smooth dough. Place in an oiled bowl, cover with oiled clingfilm (plastic wrap) and leave in a warm place for 1 hour until doubled in size.

Roll out the dough on a lightly floured surface to a large rectangle. Brush with oil and sprinkle with demerara sugar. Roll up like a Swiss (jelly) roll and cut into about ten 2.5 cm/1 in slices. Arrange on a greased baking (cookie) sheet about 1 cm/½ in apart, Cover with oiled clingfilm and leave in a warm place for 40 minutes. Bake in a preheated oven at 230°C/450°F/gas mark 8 for 15 minutes until well risen. Brush with the honey, sprinkle with walnuts and leave to cool.

Selkirk Bannock

Makes one 450 g/1 lb loaf

For the dough:

225 g/8 oz/2 cups plain (all-purpose) flour

A pinch of salt

50 g/2 oz/¼ cup lard (shortening)

150 ml/¼ pt/2/3 cup milk

15 g/½ oz fresh yeast or 20 ml/4 tsp dried yeast

50 g/2 oz/¼ cup caster (superfine) sugar

100 g/4 oz/2/3 cup sultanas (golden raisins)

For the glaze:

25 g/1 oz/2 tbsp caster (superfine) sugar

30 ml/2 tbsp water

To make the dough, mix the flour and salt. Melt the lard, add the milk and bring to blood heat. Pour on to the yeast and stir in 5 ml/1 tsp of the sugar. Leave for about 20 minutes until frothy. Make a well in the centre of the flour and pour in the yeast mixture. Gradually work in the flour and knead for 5 minutes. Cover and place in a warm place for 1 hour to rise. Turn out on to a floured work surface and work in the sultanas and the remaining sugar. Shape into a large round and place on a greased baking (cookie) sheet. Cover with oiled clingfilm (plastic wrap) and leave in a warm place until doubled in size. Bake in a preheated oven at 220°C/425°F/gas mark 7 for 15 minutes. Reduce the oven temperature to 190°C/375°F/gas mark 5 and bake for a further 25 minutes. Remove from the oven. Dissolve the sugar for the glaze in the water and brush over the hot bannock.

Sultana and Carob Bread

Makes one 900 g/2 lb loaf

150 g/5 oz/1¼ cups wholemeal (wholewheat) flour

15 ml/1 tbsp baking powder

25 g/1 oz/¼ cup carob powder

50 g/2 oz/½ cup oatmeal

50 g/2 oz/¼ cup butter or margarine, softened

175 g/6 oz/1 cup sultanas (golden raisins)

2 eggs, beaten

150 ml/¼ pt/2/3 cup milk

60 ml/4 tbsp oil

Mix together the dry ingredients. Rub in the butter or margarine, then stir in the sultanas. Beat together the eggs, milk and oil, then blend into the flour mixture to make a soft dough. Shape into a greased 900 g/2 lb loaf tin (pan) and bake in a preheated oven at 180°C/350°F/gas mark 4 for 1 hour until firm to the touch.

Sultana and Orange Loaf

Makes two 450 g/1 lb loaves

For the dough:

450 g/1 lb/4 cups wholemeal (wholewheat) flour

20 ml/4 tsp baking powder

75 g/3 oz/1/3 cup soft brown sugar

5 ml/1 tsp salt

2.5 ml/½ tsp ground mace

75 g/3 oz/1/3 cup vegetable fat (shortening)

3 egg whites

300 ml/½ pt/1¼ cups milk

For the filling:

175 g/6 oz/1½ cups wholemeal (wholewheat) cake crumbs

50 g/2 oz/½ cup ground almonds

50 g/2 oz/¼ cup soft brown sugar

100 g/4 oz/2/3 cup sultanas (golden raisins)

30 ml/2 tbsp orange juice

1 egg, lightly beaten

For the glaze:

15 ml/1 tbsp honey

To make the dough, mix together the dry ingredients and rub in the fat. Mix together the egg whites and milk and blend into the mixture until you have a soft, pliable dough. Combine the filling ingredients, using just enough of the egg to make a spreading consistency. Roll out the dough on a lightly floured surface to a 20 x 30 cm/8 x 10 in rectangle. Spread the filling over all but the top 2.5 cm/1 in along the long edge. Roll up from the opposite edge, like a Swiss (jelly) roll, and moisten the plain strip of dough to seal. Moisten each end and shape the roll into a circle, sealing the ends together. With sharp scissors, make little cuts around the top for decoration. Place on a greased baking (cookie) sheet and brush with the remaining egg. Leave to rest for 15 minutes.

Bake in a preheated oven at 230°C/450°F/gas mark 8 for 25 minutes until golden brown. Brush with the honey and leave to cool.

Sultana and Sherry Bread

Makes one 900 g/2 lb loaf

225 g/8 oz/1 cup unsalted (sweet) butter or margarine, softened

225 g/8 oz/1 cup soft brown sugar

4 eggs

45 ml/3 tbsp sweet sherry

5 ml/1 tsp vanilla essence (extract)

200 g/7 oz/1¾ cups plain (all-purpose) flour

A pinch of salt

75 g/3 oz/½ cup sultanas (golden raisins)

50 g/2 oz/1/3 cup stoned (pitted) dates, chopped

50 g/2 oz/1/3 cup dried figs, diced

50 g/2 oz/½ cup chopped mixed (candied) peel

Cream together the butter or margarine and sugar until light and fluffy. Gradually add the eggs, then the sherry and vanilla essence. Mix the flour and salt with the fruit, then fold into the mixture and mix well. Spoon into a greased and floured 900 g/2 lb loaf tin (pan) and bake in a preheated oven at 180°C/350°F/gas mark 4 for 1 hour. Leave to cool in the tin for 10 minutes, then turn out on to a wire rack to finish cooling.

Cottage Tea Bread

Makes two 450 g/1 lb loaves

For the dough:

25 g/1 oz fresh yeast or 40 ml/2½ tbsp dried yeast

15 ml/1 tbsp soft brown sugar

300 ml/½ pt/1¼ cups warm water

15 ml/1 tbsp butter or margarine

450 g/1 lb/4 cups wholemeal (wholewheat) flour

15 ml/1 tbsp milk powder (non-fat dry milk)

5 ml/1 tsp ground mixed (apple-pie) spice

2.5 ml/½ tsp salt

1 egg

175 g/6 oz/1 cup currants

100 g/4 oz/2/3 cup sultanas (golden raisins)

50 g/2 oz/1/3 cup raisins

50 g/2 oz/1/3 cup chopped mixed (candied) peel

For the glaze:

15 ml/1 tbsp lemon juice

15 ml/1 tbsp water

A pinch of ground mixed (apple-pie) spice

To make the dough, blend the yeast with the sugar with a little of the warm water and leave in a warm place for 10 minutes until frothy. Rub the butter or margarine into the flour, then stir in the milk powder, mixed spice and salt and make a well in the centre. Stir in the egg, the yeast mixture and the remaining warm water and mix to a dough. Knead until smooth and elastic. Work in the currants, sultanas, raisins and mixed peel. Place in an oiled bowl, cover with oiled clingfilm (plastic wrap) and leave in warm place for 45 minutes. Shape into two greased 450 g/1 lb loaf tins (pans). Cover with oiled clingfilm and leave in a warm place for 15 minutes. Bake in a preheated oven at 220°C/425°F/gas mark 7 for 30 minutes until golden. Remove from the tin. Mix together the glaze ingredients and brush over the hot loaves, then leave to cool.

Tea Cakes

Makes 6

15 g/½ oz fresh yeast or 20 ml/4 tsp dried yeast

300 ml/½ pt/1¼ cups warm milk

25 g/1 oz/2 tbsp caster (superfine) sugar

25 g/1 oz/2 tbsp butter or margarine

450 g/1 lb/4 cups plain (all-purpose) flour

5 ml/1 tsp salt

50 g/2 oz/1/3 cup sultanas (golden raisins)

Blend the yeast with the warm milk and a little of the sugar and leave in a warm place until frothy. Rub the butter or margarine into the flour and salt, then stir in the remaining sugar and the raisins. Stir in the yeast mixture and mix to a soft dough. Turn out on to a lightly floured surface and knead until smooth. Place in an oiled bowl, cover with oiled clingfilm (plastic wrap) and leave in a warm place until doubled in size. Knead the dough again, then divide into six pieces and roll each one into a ball. Flatten slightly on a greased baking (cookie) sheet, Cover with oiled clingfilm and leave in a warm place again until doubled in size. Bake in a preheated oven at 200°C/400°F/gas mark 6 for 20 minutes.

Potato Scones

Makes 12

50 g/2 oz/¼ cup butter or margarine

225 g/8 oz/2 cups self-raising (self-rising) flour

A pinch of salt

175 g/6 oz/¾ cup cooked mashed potato

60 ml/4 tbsp milk

Rub the butter or margarine into the flour and salt. Stir in the mashed potato and enough of the milk to make a soft dough. Roll out on a lightly floured surface to about 2.5 cm/1 in thick and cut into rounds with a biscuit (cookie) cutter. Place the scones (biscuits) on a lightly greased baking (cookie) sheet and bake in a preheated oven at 200°C/400°F/gas mark 6 for 15–20 minutes until lightly golden.

Raisin Scones

Makes 12

75 g/3 oz/½ cup raisins

225 g/8 oz/2 cups plain (all-purpose) flour

2.5 ml/½ tsp salt

15 ml/1 tbsp baking powder

25 g/1 oz/2 tbsp caster (superfine) sugar

50 g/2 oz/¼ cup butter or margarine

120 ml/4 fl oz/½ cup single (light) cream

1 egg, beaten

Soak the raisins in hot water for 30 minutes, then drain. Mix together the dry ingredients, then rub in the butter or margarine. Stir in the cream and egg to make a soft dough. Divide into three balls, then roll out until about 1 cm/½ in thick and place on a greased baking (cookie) sheet. Cut each one into quarters. Bake the scones (biscuits) in a preheated oven at 230°C/450°F/gas mark 8 for about 10 minutes until golden brown.

Treacle Scones

Makes 10

225 g/8 oz/2 cups plain (all-purpose) flour

10 ml/2 tsp baking powder

2.5 ml/½ tsp ground cinnamon

50 g/2 oz/¼ cup butter or margarine, diced

25 g/1 oz/2 tbsp caster (superfine) sugar

30 ml/2 tbsp black treacle (molasses)

150 ml/¼ pt/2/3 cup milk

Mix together the flour, baking powder and cinnamon. Rub in the butter or margarine, then stir in the sugar, treacle and enough of the milk to make a soft dough. Roll out to 1 cm/½ in thick and cut into 5 cm/2 in rounds with a biscuit (cookie) cutter. Place the scones (biscuits) on a greased baking tray and bake in a preheated oven at 220°C/425°F/gas mark 7 for 10–15 minutes until well risen and golden brown.

Treacle and Ginger Scones

Makes 12

400 g/14 oz/3½ cups plain (all-purpose) flour

50 g/2 oz/½ cup rice flour

5 ml/1 tsp bicarbonate of soda (baking soda)

2.5 ml/½ tsp cream of tartar

10 ml/2 tsp ground ginger

2.5 ml/½ tsp salt

10 ml/2 tsp caster (superfine) sugar

50 g/2 oz/¼ cup butter or margarine

30 ml/2 tbsp black treacle (molasses)

300 ml/½ pt/1¼ cups milk

Mix together the dry ingredients. Rub in the butter or margarine until the mixture resembles breadcrumbs. Stir in the treacle and enough of the milk to make a soft but not sticky dough. Knead gently on a lightly floured surface, roll out and cut into rounds with a 7.5 cm/ 3 in biscuit (cookie) cutter. Place the scones (biscuits) on a greased baking (cookie) sheet and brush with any remaining milk. Bake in a preheated oven at 220°C/425°F/gas mark 7 for 15 minutes until risen and golden brown.

Sultana Scones

Makes 12

225 g/8 oz/2 cups plain (all-purpose) flour

A pinch of salt

2.5 ml/½ tsp bicarbonate of soda (baking soda)

2.5 ml/½ tsp cream of tartar

50 g/2 oz/¼ cup butter or margarine

25 g/1 oz/2 tbsp caster (superfine) sugar

50 g/2 oz/1/3 cup sultanas (golden raisins)

7.5 ml/½ tbsp lemon juice

150 ml/¼ pt/2/3 cup milk

Mix together the flour, salt, bicar-bonate of soda and cream of tartar. Rub in the butter or margarine until the mixture resembles breadcrumbs. Stir in the sugar and sultanas. Mix the lemon juice into the milk and gradually stir into the dry ingredients until you have a soft dough. Knead lightly, then roll out to about 1 cm/½ in thick and cut into 5 cm/ 2 in rounds with a biscuit (cookie) cutter. Place the scones (biscuits) on a greased baking (cookie) sheet and bake in a preheated oven at 230°C/450°F/gas mark 8 for about 10 minutes until well risen and golden brown.

Wholemeal Treacle Scones

Makes 12

100 g/4 oz/1 cup wholemeal (wholewheat) flour

100 g/4 oz/1 cup plain (all-purpose) flour

25 g/1 oz/2 tbsp caster (superfine) sugar

2.5 ml/½ tsp cream of tartar

2.5 ml/½ tsp bicarbonate of soda (baking soda)

5 ml/1 tsp mixed (apple pie) spice

50 g/2 oz/¼ cup butter or margarine

30 ml/2 tbsp black treacle (molasses)

100 ml/3½ fl oz/6½ tbsp milk

Mix together the dry ingredients, then rub in the butter or margarine. Warm the treacle, then mix it into the ingredients with enough of the milk to make a soft dough. Roll out on a lightly floured surface to 1 cm/½ in thick and cut into rounds with a biscuit (cookie) cutter. Arrange the scones (biscuits) on a greased and floured baking (cookie) sheet and brush with milk. Bake in a preheated oven at 190°C/375°F/gas mark 5 for 20 minutes.

Yoghurt Scones

Makes 12

200 g/7 oz/1¾ cups plain (all-purpose) flour

25 g/1 oz/¼ cup rice flour

10 ml/2 tsp baking powder

A pinch of salt

15 ml/1 tbsp caster (superfine) sugar

50 g/2 oz/¼ cup butter or margarine

150 ml/¼ pt/2/3 cup plain yoghurt

Mix together the flours, baking powder, salt and sugar. Rub in the butter or margarine until the mixture resembles breadcrumbs. Stir in the yoghurt to make a soft but not sticky dough. Roll out on a floured surface to about 2 cm/¾ in thick and cut into 5 cm/ 2 in rounds with a biscuit (cookie) cutter. Place on a greased baking (cookie) sheet and bake in a preheated oven at 200°C/400°F/gas mark 6 for about 15 minutes until well risen and golden brown.

Cheese Scones

Makes 12

225 g/8 oz/2 cups plain (all-purpose) flour

2.5 ml/½ tsp salt

15 ml/1 tbsp baking powder

50 g/2 oz/¼ cup butter or margarine

100 g/4 oz/1 cup Cheddar cheese, grated

150 ml/¼ pt/2/3 cup milk

Mix together the flour, salt and baking powder. Rub in the butter or margarine until the mixture resembles breadcrumbs. Stir in the cheese. Gradually blend in the milk to make a soft dough. Knead lightly, then roll out to about 1 cm/½ in thick and cut into 5 cm/ 2 in rounds with a biscuit (cookie) cutter. Place the scones (biscuits) on a greased baking (cookie) sheet and bake in a preheated oven at 220°C/425°F/gas mark 7 for 12–15 minutes until well risen and golden on top. Serve warm or cold.

Wholemeal Herb Scones

Makes 12

100 g/4 oz/½ cup butter or margarine

175 g/6 oz/1¼ cups wholemeal (wholewheat) flour

50 g/2 oz/½ cup plain (all-purpose) flour

10 ml/2 tsp baking powder

30 ml/2 tbsp chopped fresh sage or thyme

150 ml/¼ pt/2/3 cup milk

Rub the butter or margarine into the flours and baking powder until the mixture resembles breadcrumbs. Stir in the herbs and enough of the milk to make a soft dough. Knead lightly, then roll out to about 1 cm/½ in thick and cut into 5 cm/2 in rounds with a biscuit (cookie) cutter. Place the scones (biscuits) on a greased baking (cookie) sheet and brush the tops with milk. Bake in a preheated oven at 220°C/425°F/gas mark 7 for 10 minutes until risen and golden brown.

Salami and Cheese Scones

Serves 4

50 g/2 oz/¼ cup butter or margarine

225 g/8 oz/2 cups self-raising (self-rising) flour

A pinch of salt

50 g/2 oz salami, chopped

75 g/3 oz/¾ cup Cheddar cheese, grated

75 ml/5 tbsp milk

Rub the butter or margarine into the flour and salt until the mixture resembles breadcrumbs. Stir in the salami and cheese, then add the milk and mix to a soft dough. Shape into a 20 cm/8 in round and flatten slightly. Place the scones (biscuits) on a greased baking (cookie) sheet and bake in a preheated oven at 220°C/425°F/gas mark 7 for 15 minutes until golden brown.

Wholemeal Scones

Makes 12

175 g/6 oz/1½ cups wholemeal (wholewheat) flour

50 g/2 oz/½ cup plain (all-purpose) flour

15 ml/1 tbsp baking powder

A pinch of salt

50 g/2 oz/¼ cup butter or margarine

50 g/2 oz/¼ cup caster (superfine) sugar

150 ml/¼ pt/2/3 cup milk

Mix together the flours, baking powder and salt. Rub in the butter or margarine until the mixture resembles breadcrumbs. Stir in the sugar. Gradually mix in the milk to make a soft dough. Knead lightly, then roll out to about 1 cm/½ in thick and cut into 5 cm/ 2 in rounds with a biscuit (cookie) cutter. Place the scones (biscuits) on a greased baking (cookie) sheet and bake in a preheated oven at 230°C/450°F/gas mark 8 for about 15 minutes until risen and golden brown. Serve warm.

Barbadian Conkies

Makes 12

350 g/12 oz pumpkin, grated

225 g/8 oz sweet potato, grated

1 large coconut, grated, or 225 g/8 oz 2 cups desiccated (shredded) coconut

350 g/12 oz/1½ cups soft brown sugar

5 ml/1 tsp ground mixed (apple-pie) spice

5 ml/1 tsp grated nutmeg

5 ml/1 tsp salt

5 ml/1 tsp almond essence (extract)

100 g/4 oz/2/3 cup raisins

350 g/12 oz/3 cups cornmeal

100 g/4 oz/1 cup self-raising (self-rising) flour

175 g/6 oz/¾ cup butter or margarine, melted

300 ml/½ pt/1¼ cups milk

Mix together the pumpkin, sweet potato and coconut. Stir in the sugar, spices, salt and almond essence. Add the raisins, cornmeal and flour and mix well. Mix the melted butter or margarine with the milk and fold into the dry ingredients until well blended. Place about 60 ml/4 tbsp of the mixture into a square of foil, taking care not to overfill. Fold the foil into a parcel so that it is neatly wrapped and no mixture is left exposed. Repeat with the remaining mixture. Steam the conkies on a rack over a pan of boiling water for about 1 hour until firm and cooked. Serve hot or cold.

Deep-fried Christmas Biscuits

Makes 40

50 g/2 oz/¼ cup butter or margarine

100 g/4 oz/1 cup plain (all-purpose) flour

2.5 ml/½ tsp ground cardamom

25 g/1 oz/2 tbsp caster (superfine) sugar

15 ml/1 tbsp double (heavy) cream

5 ml/1 tsp brandy

1 small egg, beaten

Oil for deep-frying

Icing (confectioners') sugar for dusting

Rub the butter or margarine into the flour and cardamom until the mixture resembles breadcrumbs. Stir in the sugar, then add the cream and brandy and enough of the egg to make a fairly stiff mixture. Cover and leave in a cool place for 1 hour.

Roll out on a lightly floured surfaced to 5 mm/¼ in thick and cut into 10 x 2.5 cm/4 x 1 in strips with a pastry cutter. Cut a slit down the middle of each strip with a sharp knife. Pull one end of the strip through the slit to make a half-bow. Deep-fry the biscuits (cookies) in batches in hot oil for about 4 minutes until golden brown and puffed. Drain on kitchen paper (paper towels) and serve sprinkled with icing sugar.

Cornmeal Cakes

Makes 12

100 g/4 oz/1 cup self-raising (self-rising) flour

100 g/4 oz/1 cup cornmeal

5 ml/1 tsp baking powder

15 g/½ oz/1 tbsp caster (superfine) sugar

2 eggs

375 ml/13 fl oz/1½ cups milk

60 ml/4 tbsp oil

Oil for shallow-frying

Mix together the dry ingredients and make a well in the centre. Beat together the eggs, milk and measured oil, then beat into the dry ingredients. Heat a little oil in a large frying pan (skillet) and fry (sauté) 60 ml/4 tbsp of the batter until bubbles appear on the top. Turn over and brown on the other side. Remove from the pan and keep warm while you continue with the remaining batter. Serve warm.

Crumpets

Makes 8

15 g/½ oz fresh yeast or 20 ml/ 4 tsp dried yeast

5 ml/1 tsp caster (superfine) sugar

300 ml/½ pt/1¼ cups milk

1 egg

250 g/9 oz/2¼ cups plain (all-purpose) flour

5 ml/1 tsp salt

Oil for greasing

Mix the yeast and sugar with a little of the milk to a paste, then blend in the remaining milk and the egg. Stir the liquid into the flour and salt and mix to a creamy, thick batter. Cover and leave in a warm place for 30 minutes until doubled in size. Heat a griddle or heavy frying pan (skillet) and grease it lightly. Place 7.5 cm/3 in baking rings on the griddle. (If you do not have baking rings, carefully cut the top and bottom off a small tin.) Pour cupfuls of the mixture into the rings and cook for about 5 minutes until the underside is browned and the top is pitted. Repeat with the remaining mixture. Serve toasted.

Doughnuts

Makes 16

300 ml/½ pt/1¼ cups warm milk

15 ml/1 tbsp dried yeast

175 g/6 oz/¾ cup caster (superfine) sugar

450 g/1 lb/4 cups strong plain (bread) flour

5 ml/1 tsp salt

50 g/2 oz/¼ cup butter or margarine

1 egg, beaten

Oil for deep-frying

5 ml/1 tsp ground cinnamon

Mix together the warm milk, yeast, 5 ml/1 tsp of the sugar and 100 g/ 4 oz/1 cup of the flour. Leave in a warm place for 20 minutes until frothy. Mix together the remaining flour, 50 g/2 oz/¼ cup of the sugar and the salt in a bowl and rub in the butter or margarine until the mixture resembles breadcrumbs. Mix in the egg and the yeast mixture and knead well to a smooth dough. Cover and leave in a warm place for 1 hour. Knead again and roll out to 2 cm/½ in thick. Cut into rings with an 8 cm/3 in cutter and cut out the centres with a 4 cm/1½ in cutter.

Place on a greased baking (cookie) sheet and leave to rise for 20 minutes. Heat the oil until almost smoking, then deep-fry the doughnuts a few at a time for a few minutes until golden. Drain well. Place the remaining sugar and the cinnamon in a bag and shake the doughnuts in the bag until well coated.

Potato Doughnuts

Makes 24

15 ml/1 tbsp dried yeast

60 ml/4 tbsp warm water

25 g/1 oz/2 tbsp caster (superfine) sugar

25 g/1 oz/2 tbsp lard (shortening)

1.5 ml/¼ tsp salt

75 g/3 oz/1/3 cup mashed potato

1 egg, beaten

120 ml/4 fl oz/½ cup milk, boiled

300 g/10 oz/2½ cups strong plain (bread) flour

Oil for deep-frying

Granulated sugar for sprinkling

Dissolve the yeast in the warm water with a teaspoon of the sugar and leave until frothy. Mix together the lard, remaining sugar and the salt. Stir in the potato, yeast mixture, egg and milk, then gradually work in the flour and mix to a smooth dough. Turn out on to a floured surface and knead well. Place in a greased bowl, cover with clingfilm (plastic wrap) and leave in a warm place for about 1 hour until doubled in size.

Knead again, then roll out to 1 cm/½ in thick. Cut into rings with an 8 cm/ 3 in cutter, then cut out the centres with a 4 cm/1½ in cutter to make doughnut shapes. Leave to rise until doubled in size. Heat the oil and deep-fry the doughnuts until golden. Sprinkle with sugar and leave to cool.

Naan Bread

Makes 6

2.5 ml/½ tsp dried yeast

60 ml/4 tbsp warm water

350 g/12 oz/3 cups plain (all-purpose) flour

10 ml/2 tsp baking powder

A pinch of salt

150 ml/¼ pt/2/3 cup plain yoghurt

Melted butter for brushing

Mix together the yeast and warm water and leave in a warm place for 10 minutes until frothy. Mix the yeast mixture into the flour, baking powder and salt, then work in the yoghurt to make a soft dough. Knead until no longer sticky. Place in an oiled bowl, cover and leave to rise for 8 hours.

Divide the dough into six pieces and roll into ovals about 5 mm/¼ in thick. Place on a greased baking (cookie) sheet and brush with melted butter. Grill (broil) under a medium grill (broiler) for about 5 minutes until slightly puffy, then turn and brush the other side with butter and grill for a further 3 minutes until lightly browned.

Oat Bannocks

Makes 4

100 g/4 oz/1 cup medium oatmeal

2.5 ml/½ tsp salt

A pinch of bicarbonate of soda (baking soda)

10 ml/2 tsp oil

60 ml/4 tsp hot water

Mix the dry ingredients in a bowl and make a well in the centre. Stir in the oil and enough of the water to make a firm dough. Turn out on to a lightly floured surface and knead until smooth. Roll out to about 5 mm/¼ in thick, tidy the edges, then cut into quarters. Heat a griddle or heavy-based frying pan (skillet) and fry (sauté) the bannocks for about 20 minutes until the corners begin to curl. Turn over and cook the other side for 6 minutes.

Pikelets

Makes 8

10 ml/2 tsp fresh yeast or 5 ml/ 1 tsp dried yeast

5 ml/1 tsp caster (superfine) sugar

300 ml/½ pt/1¼ cups milk

1 egg

225 g/8 oz/2 cups plain (all-purpose) flour

5 ml/1 tsp salt

Oil for greasing

Mix the yeast and sugar with a little of the milk to a paste, then blend in the remaining milk and the egg. Stir the liquid into the flour and salt and mix to a thin batter. Cover and leave in a warm place for 30 minutes until doubled in size. Heat a griddle or heavy frying pan (skillet) and grease it lightly. Pour cupfuls of the mixture on to the griddle and cook for about 3 minutes until the underside is browned, then turn and cook for about 2 minutes on the other side. Repeat with the remaining mixture.

Easy Drop Scones

Makes 15

100 g/4 oz/1 cup self-raising (self-rising) flour

A pinch of salt

15 ml/1 tbsp caster (superfine) sugar

1 egg

150 ml/¼ pt/2/3 cup milk

Oil for greasing

Mix together the flour, salt and sugar and make a well in the centre. Drop in the egg and gradually work in the egg and milk until you have a smooth batter. Heat a large frying pan (skillet) and oil it lightly. When hot, place spoonfuls of batter in the pan so they form rounds. Cook for about 3 minutes until the scones (biscuits) are puffed and golden on the underside, then turn over and brown the other side. Serve hot or warm.

Maple Drop Scones

Makes 30

200 g/7 oz/1¾ cups self-raising (self-rising) flour

25 g/1 oz/¼ cup rice flour

10 ml/2 tsp baking powder

25 g/1 oz/2 tbsp caster (superfine) sugar

A pinch of salt

15 ml/1 tbsp maple syrup

1 egg, beaten

200 ml/7 fl oz/scant 1 cup milk

Sunflower oil

50 g/2 oz/¼ cup butter or margarine, softened

15 ml/1 tbsp finely chopped walnuts

Mix together the flours, baking powder, sugar and salt and make a well in the centre. Add the maple syrup, egg and half the milk and beat until smooth. Stir in the remaining milk to make a thick batter. Heat a little oil in a frying pan (skillet), then pour off the excess. Drop spoonfuls of the batter into the pan and fry (sauté) until the undersides are golden. Turn and fry the other sides. Remove from the pan and keep warm while you fry the remaining scones (biscuits). Mash the butter or margarine with the nuts and top the warm scones with the flavoured butter to serve.

Griddle Scones

Makes 12

225 g/8 oz/2 cups plain (all-purpose) flour

5 ml/1 tsp bicarbonate of soda (baking soda)

10 ml/2 tsp cream of tartar

2.5 ml/½ tsp salt

25 g/1 oz/2 tbsp lard (shortening) or butter

25 g/1 oz/2 tbsp caster (superfine) sugar

150 ml/¼ pt/2/3 cup milk

Oil for greasing

Mix together the flour, bicarbonate of soda, cream of tartar and salt. Rub in the lard or butter, then stir in the sugar. Gradually blend in the milk until you have a soft dough. Cut the dough in half and knead and shape each into a flat round about 1 cm/½ in thick. Cut each round into six. Heat a griddle or large frying pan (skillet) and oil lightly. When hot, place the scones (biscuits) in the pan and cook for about 5 minutes until golden on the underside, then turn over and cook on the other side. Leave to cool on a wire rack.

Cheesy Griddle Scones

Makes 12

25 g/1 oz/2 tbsp butter or margarine, softened

100 g/4 oz/½ cup cottage cheese

5 ml/1 tsp snipped fresh chives

2 eggs, beaten

40 g/1½ oz/1/3 cup plain (all-purpose) flour

15 g/½ oz/2 tbsp rice flour

5 ml/1 tsp baking powder

15 ml/1 tbsp milk

Oil for greasing

Beat together all the ingredients except the oil to make a thick batter. Heat a little oil in a frying pan (skillet), then drain off any excess. Fry (sauté) spoonfuls of the mixture until the undersides are golden. Turn the scones (biscuits) over and fry the other side. Remove from the pan and keep warm while you fry the remaining scones

Special Scotch Pancakes

Makes 12

100 g/4 oz/1 cup plain (all-purpose) flour

10 ml/2 tsp caster (superfine) sugar

5 ml/1 tsp cream of tartar

2.5 ml/½ tsp salt

2.5 ml/½ tsp bicarbonate of soda (baking soda)

1 egg

5 ml/1 tsp golden (light corn) syrup

120 ml/4 fl oz/½ cup warm milk

Oil for greasing

Mix together the dry ingredients and make a well in the centre. Beat the egg with the syrup and milk and mix into the flour mixture until you have a very thick batter. Cover and leave to stand for about 15 minutes until the mixture bubbles. Heat a large griddle or heavy-based frying pan (skillet) and grease it lightly. Drop small spoonfuls of the batter on to the griddle and cook one side for about 3 minutes until the underside is golden, then turn and cook the other side for about 2 minutes. Wrap the pancakes in a warm tea towel (dish cloth) while you cook the remaining batter. Serve fresh and buttered, toasted or fried (sautéed).

Fruit Scotch Pancakes

Makes 12

100 g/4 oz/1 cup plain (all-purpose) flour

10 ml/2 tsp caster (superfine) sugar

5 ml/1 tsp cream of tartar

2.5 ml/½ tsp salt

2.5 ml/½ tsp bicarbonate of soda (baking soda)

100 g/4 oz/2/3 cup raisins

1 egg

5 ml/1 tsp golden (light corn) syrup

120 ml/4 fl oz/½ cup warm milk

Oil for greasing

Mix together the dry ingredients and raisins and make a well in the centre. Beat the egg with the syrup and milk and mix into the flour mixture until you have a very thick batter. Cover and leave to stand for about 15 minutes until the mixture bubbles. Heat a large griddle or heavy-based frying pan (skillet) and grease it lightly. Drop small spoonfuls of the batter on to the griddle and cook one side for about 3 minutes until the underside is golden, then turn and cook the other side for about 2 minutes. Wrap the pancakes in a warm tea towel (dish cloth) while you cook the remainder. Serve fresh and buttered, toasted or fried (sautéed).

Orange Scotch Pancakes

Makes 12

100 g/4 oz/1 cup plain (all-purpose) flour

10 ml/2 tsp caster (superfine) sugar

5 ml/1 tsp cream of tartar

2.5 ml/½ tsp salt

2.5 ml/½ tsp bicarbonate of soda (baking soda)

10 ml/2 tsp grated orange rind

1 egg

5 ml/1 tsp golden (light corn) syrup

120 ml/4 fl oz/½ cup warm milk

A few drops of orange essence (extract)

Oil for greasing

Mix together the dry ingredients and orange rind and make a well in the centre. Beat the egg with the syrup, milk and orange essence and mix into the flour mixture until you have a very thick batter. Cover and leave to stand for about 15 minutes until the mixture bubbles. Heat a large griddle or heavy-based frying pan (skillet) and grease it lightly. Drop small spoonfuls of the batter on to the griddle and cook one side for about 3 minutes until the underside is golden, then turn and cook the other side for about 2 minutes. Wrap the pancakes in a warm tea towel (dish cloth) while you cook the remainder. Serve fresh and buttered, toasted or fried (sautéed).

Singing Hinny

Makes 12

225 g/8 oz/2 cups plain (all-purpose) flour

2.5 ml/½ tsp salt

2.5 ml/½ tsp baking powder

50 g/2 oz/¼ cup lard (shortening)

50 g/2 oz/¼ cup butter or margarine

100 g/4 oz/2/3 cup currants

120 ml/4 fl oz/½ cup milk

Oil for greasing

Mix together the dry ingredients, then rub in the lard and butter or margarine until the mixture resembles breadcrumbs. Stir in the currants and make a well in the centre. Mix in enough of the milk to make a stiff dough. Roll out on a lightly floured surface to about 1 cm/½ in thick and prick the top with a fork. Heat a griddle or heavy-based frying pan (skillet) and grease it lightly. Cook the cake for about 5 minutes until the underside is golden, then turn and cook the other side for about 4 minutes. Serve split and buttered.

Welsh Cakes

Serves 4

225 g/8 oz/2 cups plain (all-purpose) flour

5 ml/1 tsp baking powder

2.5 ml/½ tsp ground mixed (apple-pie) spice

50 g/2 oz/¼ cup butter or margarine

50 g/2 oz/¼ cup lard (shortening)

75 g/3 oz/1/3 cup caster (superfine) sugar

50 g/2 oz/1/3 cup currants

1 egg, beaten

30–45 ml/2–3 tbsp milk

Mix together the flour, baking powder and mixed spice in a bowl. Rub in the butter or margarine and lard until the mixture resembles breadcrumbs. Stir in the sugar and currants. Stir in the egg and enough of the milk to make a stiff dough. Roll out on a floured board to 5 mm/¼ in thick and cut into 7.5 cm/3 in rounds. Bake on a greased griddle for about 4 minutes on each side until golden brown.

Welsh Pancakes

Makes 12

175 g/6 oz/1½ cups plain (all-purpose) flour

2.5 ml/½ tsp cream of tartar

2.5 ml/½ tsp bicarbonate of soda (baking soda)

50 g/2 oz/¼ cup caster (superfine) sugar

25 g/1 oz/2 tbsp butter or margarine

1 egg, beaten

120 ml/4 fl oz/½ cup milk

2.5 ml/½ tsp vinegar

Oil for greasing

Mix together the dry ingredients and stir in the sugar. Rub in the butter or margarine and make a well in the centre. Mix in the egg and just enough of the milk to make a thin batter. Stir in the vinegar. Heat a griddle or heavy-based frying pan (skillet) and grease it lightly. Drop large spoonfuls of batter into the pan and fry (sauté) for about 3 minutes until golden on the underside. Turn and cook the other side for about 2 minutes. Serve hot and buttered.

Mexican Spiced Corn Bread

Makes 8 rolls

225 g/8 oz/2 cups self-raising (self-rising) flour

5 ml/1 tsp chilli powder

2.5 ml/½ tsp bicarbonate of soda (baking soda)

200 g/7 oz/1 small can creamed sweetcorn (corn)

15 ml/1 tbsp curry paste

250 ml/8 fl oz/1 cup plain yoghurt

Oil for shallow-frying

Mix together the flour, chilli powder and bicarbonate of soda. Stir in the remaining ingredients except the oil and mix to a soft dough. Turn out on to a lightly floured surface and knead gently until smooth. Cut into eight pieces and pat each one into a 13 cm/5 in round. Heat the oil in a heavy-based frying pan (skillet) and fry (sauté) the corn breads for 2 minutes on each side until browned and lightly puffed.

Swedish Flat Bread

Makes 4

225 g/8 oz/2 cups wholemeal (wholewheat) flour

225 g/8 oz/2 cups rye or barley flour

5 ml/1 tsp salt

About 250 ml/8 fl oz/1 cup lukewarm water

Oil for greasing

Mix the flours and salt in a bowl, then gradually work in the water until you have a firm dough. You may need a little more or less water, depending on the flour you use. Beat well until the mixture leaves the sides of the bowl, then turn out on to a lightly floured surface and knead for 5 minutes. Divide the dough into four and roll out thinly to 20 cm/8 in rounds. Heat a griddle or large frying pan (skillet) and oil it lightly. Fry (sauté) one or two breads at a time for about 15 minutes on each side until golden.

Steamed Rye and Sweetcorn Bread

Makes one 23 cm/9 in loaf

175 g/6 oz/1½ cups rye flour

175 g/6 oz/1½ cups wholemeal (wholewheat) flour

100 g/4 oz/1 cup oatmeal

10 ml/2 tsp bicarbonate of soda (baking soda)

5 ml/1 tsp salt

450 ml/¾ pt/2 cups milk

175 g/6 oz/½ cup black treacle (molasses)

10 ml/2 tsp lemon juice

Mix together the flours, oatmeal, bicarbonate of soda and salt. Warm the milk, treacle and lemon juice until lukewarm, then stir into the dry ingredients. Spoon into a greased 23 cm/ 9 in pudding bowl and cover with pleated foil. Place in a large pan and fill with enough hot water to come half-way up the sides of the tin. Cover and boil for 3 hours, topping up with boiling water as necessary. Leave overnight before serving.

Steamed Sweetcorn Bread

Makes two 450 g/1 lb loaves

175 g/6 oz/1½ cups plain (all-purpose) flour

225 g/8 oz/2 cups cornmeal

15 ml/1 tbsp baking powder

A pinch of salt

3 eggs

45 ml/3 tbsp oil

150 ml/¼ pt/2/3 cup milk

300 g/11 oz canned sweetcorn (corn), drained and mashed

Mix together the flour, cornmeal, baking powder and salt. Beat together the eggs, oil and milk, then stir into the dry ingredients with the sweetcorn. Spoon into two greased 450 g/1 lb loaf tins (pans) and place in a large pan filled with enough boiling water to come half-way up the sides of the tins. Cover and simmer for 2 hours, topping up with boiling water as necessary. Leave to cool in the tins before turning out and slicing.

Wholemeal Chapatis

Makes 12

225 g/8 oz/2 cups wholemeal (wholewheat) flour

5 ml/1 tsp salt

150 ml/¼ pt/2/3 cup water

Mix the flour and salt in a bowl, then gradually work in the water until you have a firm dough. Divide into 12 and roll out thinly on a floured surface. Grease a heavy-based frying pan (skillet) or griddle and fry (sauté) a few chapatis at a time over a moderate heat until brown underneath. Turn over and cook the other side until lightly browned. Keep the chapatis warm while you fry the remainder. Serve buttered on one side, if liked.

Wholemeal Puris

Makes 8

100 g/4 oz/1 cup wholemeal (wholewheat) flour

100 g/4 oz/1 cup plain (all-purpose) flour

2.5 ml/½ tsp salt

25 g/1 oz/2 tbsp butter or margarine, melted

150 ml/¼ pt/2/3 cup water

Oil for deep-frying

Mix together the flours and salt and make a well in the centre. Pour in the butter or margarine. Gradually add the water, mixing to a firm dough. Knead for 5–10 minutes, then cover with a damp cloth and leave to stand for 15 minutes.

Divide the dough into eight and roll each one into a thin 13 cm/5 in round. Heat the oil in a large heavy-based frying pan (skillet) and fry (sauté) the puris one or two at a time until they puff up and are crisp and golden. Drain on kitchen paper (paper towels).

Almond Biscuits

Makes 24

100 g/4 oz/½ cup butter or margarine, softened

50 g/2 oz/¼ cup caster (superfine) sugar

100 g/4 oz/1 cup self-raising (self-rising) flour

25 g/1 oz/¼ cup ground almonds

A few drops of almond essence (extract)

Cream together the butter or margarine and sugar until light and fluffy. Work in the flour, ground almonds and almond essence to a stiff mixture. Shape into large walnut-sized balls and arrange well apart on a greased baking (cookie) sheet, then press down lightly with a fork to flatten. Bake the biscuits (cookies) in a preheated oven at 180°C/350°F/gas mark 4 for 15 minutes until golden brown.

Almond Curls

Makes 30

100 g/4 oz/1 cup flaked (slivered) almonds

100 g/4 oz/½ cup butter or margarine

100 g/4 oz/½ cup caster (superfine) sugar

30 ml/2 tbsp milk

15–30 ml/1–2 tbsp plain (all-purpose) flour

Place the almonds, butter or margarine, sugar and milk in a pan with 15 ml/ 1 tbsp of the flour. Heat gently, stirring, until blended, adding the remaining flour if necessary to make the mixture hold together. Place spoonfuls well apart on a greased and floured baking (cookie) sheet and bake in a preheated oven at 180°C/350°F/gas mark 4 for 8 minutes until light brown. Leave to cool on the baking sheet for about 30 seconds, then shape them into curls around the handle of a wooden spoon. If they become too cool to shape, return them to the oven for a few seconds to warm again before shaping the remainder.

Almond Rings

Makes 24

100 g/4 oz/½ cup butter or margarine, softened

100 g/4 oz/½ cup caster (superfine) sugar

1 egg, separated

225 g/8 oz/2 cups plain (all-purpose) flour

5 ml/1 tsp baking powder

5 ml/1 tsp grated lemon rind

50 g/2 oz/½ cup flaked (slivered) almonds

Caster (superfine) sugar for sprinkling

Cream together the butter or margarine and sugar until light and fluffy. Gradually beat in the egg yolk, then work in the flour, baking powder and lemon rind, finishing with your hands until the mixture binds together. Roll out to 5 mm/ ¼ in thick and cut into 6 cm/2¼ in rounds with a biscuit (cookie) cutter, then cut out the centres with a 2 cm/¾ in cutter. Place the biscuits well apart on a greased baking (cookie) sheet and prick them with a fork. Bake in a preheated oven at 180°C/350°F/ gas mark 4 for 10 minutes. Brush with egg white, sprinkle with the almonds and sugar, then return to the oven for a further 5 minutes until pale golden.

Mediterranean Almond Cracks

Makes 24

2 eggs, separated

175 g/6 oz/1 cup icing (confectioners') sugar, sifted

10 ml/2 tsp baking powder

Grated rind of ½ lemon

A few drops of vanilla essence (extract)

400 g/14 oz/3½ cups ground almonds

Beat the yolks and one egg white with the sugar until pale and fluffy. Beat in all the remaining ingredients and mix to a stiff dough. Roll into walnut-sized balls and arrange on a greased baking (cookie) sheet, pressing down gently to flatten them. Bake in a preheated oven at 180°C/350°F/gas mark 4 for 15 minutes until golden and cracked on the surface.

Almond and Chocolate Cookies

Makes 24

50 g/2 oz/¼ cup butter or margarine, softened

75 g/3 oz/1/3 cup caster (superfine) sugar

1 small egg, beaten

100 g/4 oz/1 cup plain (all-purpose) flour

2.5 ml/½ tsp baking powder

25 g/1 oz/¼ cup ground almonds

25 g/1 oz/¼ cup plain (semi-sweet) chocolate, grated

Cream together the butter or margarine and sugar until light and fluffy. Gradually beat in the egg, then stir in the remaining ingredients to make a fairly stiff dough. If the mixture is too moist, add a little more flour. Wrap in clingfilm (plastic wrap) and chill for 30 minutes.

> Roll the dough into a cylinder shape and cut into 1 cm/½ in slices. Arrange, well apart, on a greased baking (cookie) sheet and bake in a preheated oven at 190°C/ 375°F/gas mark 5 for 10 minutes.

Amish Fruit and Nut Biscuits

Makes 24

100 g/4 oz/½ cup butter or margarine, softened

175 g/6 oz/¾ cup caster (superfine) sugar

1 egg

75 ml/5 tbsp milk

75 g/3 oz/¼ cup black treacle (molasses)

250 g/9 oz/2¼ cups plain (all-purpose) flour

10 ml/2 tsp baking powder

15 ml/1 tbsp ground cinnamon

10 ml/2 tsp bicarbonate of soda (baking soda)

2.5 ml/½ tsp grated nutmeg

50 g/2 oz/½ cup medium oatmeal

50 g/2 oz/1/3 cup raisins

25 g/1 oz/¼ cup chopped mixed nuts

Cream together the butter or margarine and sugar until light and fluffy. Gradually beat in the egg, then the milk and treacle. Fold in the remaining ingredients and mix to a stiff dough. Add a little more milk if the mixture is too stiff to work, or a little more flour if it is too sticky; the texture will vary depending on the flour you use. Roll out the dough to about 5 mm/¼ in thick and cut into rounds with a biscuit (cookie) cutter. Place on a greased baking (cookie) sheet and bake in a preheated oven at 180°C/ 350°F/gas mark 4 for 10 minutes until golden.

Anise Biscuits

Makes 16

175 g/6 oz/¾ cup caster (superfine) sugar

2 egg whites

1 egg

100 g/4 oz/1 cup plain (all-purpose) flour

5 ml/1 tsp ground anise

Beat together the sugar, egg whites and egg for 10 minutes. Gradually beat in the flour and stir in the anise. Spoon the mixture into a 450 g/1 lb loaf tin (pan) and bake in a preheated oven at 180°C/ 350°F/gas mark 4 for 35 minutes until a skewer inserted in the centre comes out clean. Remove from the tin and cut into 1 cm/½ in slices. Place the biscuits (cookies) on their sides on a greased baking (cookie) sheet and return to the oven for a further 10 minutes, turning half-way through cooking.

Banana, Oat and Orange Juice Cookies

Makes 24

100 g/4 oz/½ cup butter or margarine, softened

100 g/4 oz ripe bananas, mashed

120 ml/4 fl oz/½ cup orange juice

4 egg whites, lightly beaten

10 ml/2 tsp vanilla essence (extract)

5 ml/1 tsp finely grated orange rind

225 g/8 oz/2 cups rolled oats

225 g/8 oz/2 cups plain (all-purpose) flour

5 ml/1 tsp bicarbonate of soda (baking soda)

5 ml/1 tsp grated nutmeg

A pinch of salt

Beat the butter or margarine until soft, then stir in the bananas and orange juice. Mix together the egg whites, vanilla essence and orange rind, then stir into the banana mixture, followed by the remaining ingredients. Drop spoonfuls on to baking (cookie) sheets and bake in a preheated oven at 180°C/350°F/gas mark 4 for 20 minutes until golden brown.

Basic Biscuits

Makes 40

100 g/4 oz/½ cup butter or margarine, softened

100 g/4 oz/½ cup caster (superfine) sugar

1 egg, beaten

5 ml/1 tsp vanilla essence (extract)

225 g/8 oz/2 cups plain (all-purpose) flour

Cream together the butter or margarine and sugar until light and fluffy. Gradually beat in the egg and vanilla essence, then fold in the flour and knead to a smooth dough. Roll into a ball, wrap in clingfim (plastic wrap) and chill for 1 hour.

Roll out the dough to 5 mm/¼ in thick and cut into rounds with a biscuit (cookie) cutter. Arrange on a greased baking (cookie) sheet and bake in a preheated oven at 200°C/400°F/gas mark 6 for 10 minutes until golden. Leave to cool on the sheet for 5 minutes before transferring to a wire rack to finish cooling.

Crunchy Bran Biscuits

Makes 16

100 g/4 oz/1 cup wholemeal (wholewheat) flour

100 g/4 oz/½ cup soft brown sugar

25 g/1 oz/¼ cup rolled oats

25 g/1 oz/½ cup bran

5 ml/1 tsp bicarbonate of soda (baking soda)

5 ml/1 tsp ground ginger

100 g/4 oz/½ cup butter or margarine

15 ml/1 tbsp golden (light corn) syrup

15 ml/1 tbsp milk

Mix together the dry ingredients. Melt the butter with the syrup and milk, then mix into the dry ingredients to make a stiff dough. Place spoonfuls of the biscuit (cookie) mixture on a greased baking (cookie) sheet and bake in a preheated oven at 160°C/325°F/gas mark 3 for 15 minutes until golden brown.

Sesame Bran Biscuits

Makes 12

225 g/8 oz/2 cups wholemeal (wholewheat) flour

5 ml/1 tsp baking powder

25 g/1 oz/½ cup bran

A pinch of salt

50 g/2 oz/¼ cup butter or margarine

45 ml/3 tbsp soft brown sugar

45 ml/3 tbsp sultanas (golden raisins)

1 egg, lightly beaten

120 ml/4 fl oz/½ cup milk

45 ml/3 tbsp sesame seeds

Mix together the flour, baking powder, bran and salt, then rub in the butter or margarine until the mixture resembles breadcrumbs. Stir in the sugar and sultanas, then mix in the egg and enough of the milk to make a soft but not sticky dough. Roll out to 1 cm/½ in thick and cut into rounds with a biscuit (cookie) cutter. Place on a greased baking (cookie) sheet, brush with milk and sprinkle with sesame seeds. Bake in a preheated oven at 220°C/425°F/gas mark 7 for 10 minutes until golden brown.

Brandy Biscuits with Caraway

Makes 30

25 g/1 oz/2 tbsp butter or margarine, softened

75 g/3 oz/1/3 cup soft brown sugar

½ egg

10 ml/2 tsp brandy

175 g/6 oz/1½ cups plain (all-purpose) flour

10 ml/2 tsp caraway seeds

5 ml/1 tsp baking powder

A pinch of salt

Cream together the butter or margarine and sugar until light and fluffy. Gradually beat in the egg and the brandy, then stir in the remaining ingredients and mix to a stiff dough. Wrap in clingfilm (plastic wrap) and chill for 30 minutes.

Roll out the dough on a lightly floured surface to about 3 mm/1/8 in thick and cut into rounds with a biscuit (cookie) cutter. Place the biscuits on a greased baking (cookie) sheet and bake in a preheated oven at 200°C/400°F/gas mark 6 for 10 minutes.

Brandy Snaps

Makes 30

100 g/4 oz/½ cup butter or margarine

100 g/4 oz/1/3 cup golden (light corn) syrup

100 g/4 oz/½ cup demerara sugar

100 g/4 oz/1 cup plain (all-purpose) flour

5 ml/1 tsp ground ginger

5 ml/1 tsp lemon juice

Melt the butter or margarine, syrup and sugar in a pan. Leave to cool slightly, then stir in the flour and ginger, then the lemon juice. Drop teaspoonfuls of the mixture 10 cm/4 in apart on to greased baking (cookie) sheets and bake in a preheated oven at 180°C/350°F/gas mark 4 for 8 minutes until golden brown. Leave to cool for a minute, then lift from the baking sheet with a slice and roll around the greased handle of a wooden spoon. Slip off the spoon handle and leave to cool on a wire rack. If the snaps harden too much before you shape them, put them back in the oven for a minute to warm and soften.

Butter Biscuits

Makes 24

100 g/4 oz/½ cup butter or margarine, softened

50 g/2 oz/¼ cup caster (superfine) sugar

Grated rind of 1 lemon

150 g/5 oz/1¼ cups self-raising (self-rising) flour

Cream together the butter or margarine and sugar until light and fluffy. Work in the lemon rind, then mix in the flour to a stiff mixture. Shape into large walnut-sized balls and arrange well apart on a greased baking (cookie) sheet, then press down lightly with a fork to flatten. Bake the biscuits (cookies) in a preheated oven at 180°C/350°F/gas mark 4 for 15 minutes until golden brown.

Butterscotch Biscuits

Makes 40

100 g/4 oz/½ cup butter or margarine, softened

100 g/4 oz/½ cup dark soft brown sugar

1 egg, beaten

1.5 ml/¼ tsp vanilla essence (extract)

225 g/8 oz/2 cups plain (all-purpose) flour

7.5 ml/1½ tsp baking powder

A pinch of salt

Cream together the butter or margarine and sugar until light and fluffy. Gradually beat in the egg and vanilla essence. Mix in the flour, baking powder and salt. Shape the dough into three rolls about 5 cm/2 in in diameter, wrap in clingfilm (plastic wrap) and chill for 4 hours or overnight.

Cut into 3 mm/1/8 in thick slices and arrange on ungreased baking (cookie) sheets. Bake the biscuits (cookies) in a preheated oven at 190°C/375°F/gas mark 5 for 10 minutes until lightly browned.

Caramel Biscuits

Makes 30

50 g/2 oz/¼ cup butter or margarine, softened

50 g/2 oz/¼ cup lard (shortening)

225 g/8 oz/1 cup soft brown sugar

1 egg, lightly beaten

175 g/6 oz/1½ cups plain (all-purpose) flour

1.5 ml/¼ tsp bicarbonate of soda (baking soda)

1.5 ml/¼ tsp cream of tartar

A pinch of grated nutmeg

10 ml/2 tsp water

2.5 ml/½ tsp vanilla essence (extract)

Cream together the butter or margarine, lard and sugar until light and fluffy. Gradually beat in the egg. Fold in the flour, bicarbonate of soda, cream of tartar and nutmeg, then add the water and vanilla essence and mix to a soft dough. Roll into a sausage shape, wrap in clingfilm (plastic wrap) and chill for at least 30 minutes, preferably longer.

Cut the dough into 1 cm/½ in slices and arrange on a greased baking (cookie) sheet. Bake the biscuits (cookies) in a preheated oven at 180°C/350°F/gas mark 4 for 10 minutes until golden.

Carrot and Walnut Cookies

Makes 48

175 g/6 oz/¾ cup butter or margarine, softened

100 g/4 oz/½ cup soft brown sugar

50 g/2 oz/¼ cup caster (superfine) sugar

1 egg, lightly beaten

225 g/8 oz/2 cups plain (all-purpose) flour

5 ml/1 tsp baking powder

2.5 ml/½ tsp salt

100 g/4 oz/½ cup mashed cooked carrots

100 g/4 oz/1 cup walnuts, chopped

Cream together the butter or margarine and sugars until light and fluffy. Gradually beat in the egg, then fold in the flour, baking powder and salt. Fold in the mashed carrots and walnuts. Drop small spoonfuls on to a greased baking (cookie) sheet and bake in a preheated oven at 200°C/400°F/gas mark 6 for 10 minutes.

Orange-iced Carrot and Walnut Biscuits

Makes 48

For the biscuits (cookies):

175 g/6 oz/¾ cup butter or margarine, softened

100 g/4 oz/½ cup caster (superfine) sugar

50 g/2 oz/¼ cup soft brown sugar

1 egg, lightly beaten

225 g/8 oz/2 cups plain (all-purpose) flour

5 ml/1 tsp baking powder

2.5 ml/½ tsp salt

5 ml/1 tsp vanilla essence (extract)

100 g/4 oz /½ cup mashed cooked carrots

100 g/4 oz/1 cup walnuts, chopped

For the icing (frosting):

175 g/6 oz/1 cup icing (confectioners') sugar, sifted

10 ml/2 tsp grated orange rind

30 ml/2 tbsp orange juice

To make the biscuits, cream together the butter or margarine and sugars until light and fluffy. Gradually beat in the egg, then fold in the flour, baking powder and salt. Fold in the vanilla essence, mashed carrots and walnuts. Drop small spoonfuls on to a greased baking (cookie) sheet and bake in a preheated oven at 200°C/400°F/gas mark 6 for 10 minutes.

To make the icing, place the icing sugar in a bowl, stir in the orange rind and make a well in the centre. Gradually work in the orange juice a little at a time until you have a smooth but fairly thick icing. Spread over the biscuits while they are still warm, then leave to cool and set.

Cherry Biscuits

Makes 48

100 g/4 oz/½ cup butter or margarine, softened

100 g/4 oz/½ cup caster (superfine) sugar

1 egg, beaten

5 ml/1 tsp vanilla essence (extract)

225 g/8 oz/2 cups plain (all-purpose) flour

50 g/2 oz/¼ cup glacé (candied) cherries, chopped

Cream together the butter or margarine and sugar until light and fluffy. Gradually beat in the egg and vanilla essence, then fold in the flour and cherries and knead to a smooth dough. Roll into a ball, wrap in clingfim (plastic wrap) and chill for 1 hour.

Roll out the dough to 5 mm/¼ in thick and cut into rounds with a biscuit (cookie) cutter. Arrange on a greased baking (cookie) sheet and bake in a preheated oven at 200°C/400°F/gas mark 6 for 10 minutes until golden. Leave to cool on the sheet for 5 minutes before transferring to a wire rack to finish cooling.

Cherry and Almond Rings

Makes 24

100 g/4 oz/½ cup butter or margarine, softened

100 g/4 oz/½ cup caster (superfine) sugar, plus extra for sprinkling

1 egg, separated

225 g/8 oz/2 cups plain (all-purpose) flour

5 ml/1 tsp baking powder

5 ml/1 tsp grated lemon rind

60 ml/4 tbsp glacé (candied) cherries

50 g/2 oz/½ cup flaked (slivered) almonds

Cream together the butter or margarine and sugar until light and fluffy. Gradually beat in the egg yolk, then work in the flour, baking powder, lemon rind and cherries, finishing with your hands until the mixture binds together. Roll out to 5 mm/¼ in thick and cut into 6 cm/ 2¼ in rounds with a biscuit (cookie) cutter, then cut out the centres with a 2 cm/¾ in cutter. Place the biscuits well apart on a greased baking (cookie) sheet and prick them with a fork. Bake in a preheated oven at 180°C/350°F/gas mark 4 for 10 minutes. Brush with egg white and sprinkle with the almonds and sugar, then return to the oven for a further 5 minutes until pale golden.

Chocolate Butter Biscuits

Makes 24

100 g/4 oz/½ cup butter or margarine

50 g/2 oz/¼ cup caster (superfine) sugar

100 g/4 oz/1 cup self-raising (self-rising) flour

30 ml/2 tbsp cocoa (unsweetened chocolate) powder

Cream together the butter or margarine and sugar until light and fluffy. Work in the flour and cocoa to a stiff mixture. Shape into large walnut-sized balls and arrange well apart on a greased baking (cookie) sheet, then press down lightly with a fork to flatten. Bake the biscuits (cookies) in a preheated oven at 180°C/350°F/gas mark 4 for 15 minutes until brown.

Chocolate and Cherry Rolls

Makes 24

100 g/4 oz/½ cup butter or margarine, softened

100 g/4 oz/½ cup caster (superfine) sugar

1 egg

2.5 ml/½ tsp vanilla essence (extract)

225 g/8 oz/2 cups plain (all-purpose) flour

5 ml/1 tsp baking powder

A pinch of salt

25 g/1 oz/¼ cup cocoa (unsweetened chocolate) powder

25 g/1 oz/2 tbsp glacé (candied) cherries, chopped

Cream together the butter and sugar until light and fluffy. Gradually beat in the egg and vanilla essence, then stir in the flour, baking powder and salt to make a stiff dough. Divide the dough in half and mix the cocoa into one half and the cherries into the other half. Wrap in clingfilm (plastic wrap) and chill for 30 minutes.

Roll out each piece of dough to a rectangle about 3 mm/1/8 in thick, then place one on top of the other and press together gently with the rolling pin. Roll up from the longest side and press together gently. Cut into 1 cm/½ in thick slices and arrange, well apart, on a greased baking (cookie) sheet. Bake in a preheated oven at 200°C/400°F/gas mark 6 for 10 minutes.

Chocolate Chip Biscuits

Makes 24

75 g/3 oz/1/3 cup butter or margarine

175 g/6 oz/1½ cups plain (all-purpose) flour

5 ml/1 tsp baking powder

A pinch of bicarbonate of soda (baking soda)

50 g/2 oz/¼ cup soft brown sugar

45 ml/3 tbsp golden (light corn) syrup

100 g/4 oz/1 cup chocolate chips

Rub the butter or margarine into the flour, baking powder and bicarbonate of soda until the mixture resembles breadcrumbs. Stir in the sugar, syrup and chocolate chips and mix to smooth dough. Shape into small balls and arrange on a greased baking (cookie) sheet, pressing down lightly to flatten. Bake the biscuits (cookies) in a preheated oven at 190°C/375°F/gas mark 5 for 15 minutes until golden.

Chocolate and Banana Chip Cookies

Makes 24

75 g/3 oz/1/3 cup butter or margarine

175 g/6 oz/1½ cups plain (all-purpose) flour

5 ml/1 tsp baking powder

2.5 ml/½ tsp bicarbonate of soda (baking soda)

50 g/2 oz/¼ cup soft brown sugar

45 ml/3 tbsp golden (light corn) syrup

50 g/2 oz/½ cup chocolate chips

50 g/2 oz/½ cup dried banana chips, coarsely chopped

Rub the butter or margarine into the flour, baking powder and bicarbonate of soda until the mixture resembles breadcrumbs. Stir in the sugar, syrup and chocolate and banana chips and mix to smooth dough. Shape into small balls and arrange on a greased baking (cookie) sheet, pressing down lightly to flatten. Bake the biscuits (cookies) in a preheated oven at 190°C/375°F/gas mark 5 for 15 minutes until golden.

Chocolate and Nut Bites

Makes 24

50 g/2 oz/¼ cup butter or margarine, softened

175 g/6 oz/¾ cup caster (superfine) sugar

1 egg

5 ml/1 tsp vanilla essence (extract)

25 g/1 oz/¼ cup plain (semi-sweet) chocolate, melted

100 g/4 oz/1 cup plain (all-purpose) flour

5 ml/1 tsp baking powder

A pinch of salt

30 ml/2 tbsp milk

25 g/1 oz/¼ cup chopped mixed nuts

Icing (confectioners') sugar, sifted, for dusting

Cream together the butter or margarine and caster sugar until light and fluffy. Gradually beat in the egg and vanilla essence, then stir in the chocolate. Mix together the flour, baking powder and salt and blend into the mixture alternately with the milk. Stir in the nuts, cover and chill for 3 hours.

Roll the mixture into 3 cm/1½ in balls and roll in the icing sugar. Arrange on a lightly greased baking (cookie) sheet and bake in a preheated oven at 180°C/350°F/ gas mark 4 for 15 minutes until lightly browned. Serve dusted with icing sugar.

American Chocolate Chip Cookies

Makes 20

225 g/8 oz/1 cup lard (shortening)

225 g/8 oz/1 cup soft brown sugar

100 g/4 oz/½ cup granulated sugar

5 ml/1 tsp vanilla essence (extract)

2 eggs, lightly beaten

175 g/6 oz/1½ cups plain (all-purpose) flour

5 ml/1 tsp salt

5 ml/1 tsp bicarbonate of soda (baking soda)

225 g/8 oz/2 cups rolled oats

350 g/12 oz/3 cups chocolate chips

Cream together the lard, sugars and vanilla essence until light and fluffy. Gradually beat in the eggs. Stir in the flour, salt, bicarbonate of soda and oats, then stir in the chocolate chips. Place spoonfuls of the mixture on to greased baking (cookie) sheets and bake in a preheated oven at 180°C/350°F/gas mark 4 for about 10 minutes until golden.

Chocolate Creams

Makes 24

175 g/6 oz/¾ cup butter or margarine, softened

175 g/6 oz/¾ cup caster (superfine) sugar

225 g/8 oz/2 cups self-raising (self-rising) flour

75 g/3 oz/¾ cup desiccated (shredded) coconut

100 g/4 oz/4 cups cornflakes, crushed

25 g/1 oz/¼ cup cocoa (unsweetened chocolate) powder

60 ml/4 tbsp boiling water

100 g/4 oz/1 cup plain (semi-sweet) chocolate

Cream together the butter or margarine and sugar, then stir in the flour, coconut and cornflakes. Blend the cocoa with the boiling water, then stir into the mixture. Roll into 2.5 cm/1 in balls, arrange on a greased baking (cookie) sheet and press lightly with a fork to flatten. Bake in a preheated oven at 180°C/350°F/gas mark 4 for 15 minutes until golden.

Melt the chocolate in a heatproof bowl over a pan of gently simmering water. Spread over the top of half the biscuits (cookies) and press the other half on top. Leave to cool.

Chocolate Chip and Hazelnut Cookies

Makes 16

200 g/7 oz/scant 1 cup butter or margarine, softened

50 g/2 oz/¼ cup caster (superfine) sugar

100 g/4 oz/½ cup soft brown sugar

10 ml/2 tsp vanilla essence (extract)

1 egg, beaten

275 g/10 oz/2½ cups plain (all-purpose) flour

50 g/2 oz/½ cup cocoa (unsweetened chocolate) powder

5 ml/1 tsp baking powder

75 g/3 oz/¾ cup hazelnuts

225 g/8 oz/2 cups white chocolate, chopped

Beat together the butter or margarine, sugars and vanilla essence until pale and fluffy, then beat in the egg. Stir in the flour, cocoa and baking powder. Stir in the nuts and chocolate until the mixture binds together. Shape into 16 balls and space out evenly on a greased and lined baking (cookie) sheet, then flatten slightly with the back of a spoon. Bake in a preheated oven at 160°C/325°F/gas mark 3 for about 15 minutes until just set but still slightly soft.

Chocolate and Nutmeg Biscuits

Makes 24

50 g/2 oz/¼ cup butter or margarine, softened

100 g/4 oz/½ cup caster (superfine) sugar

15 ml/1 tbsp cocoa (unsweetened chocolate) powder

1 egg yolk

2.5 ml/½ tsp vanilla essence (extract)

150 g/5 oz/1¼ cups plain (all-purpose) flour

5 ml/1 tsp baking powder

A pinch of grated nutmeg

60 ml/4 tbsp soured (dairy sour) cream

Cream together the butter or margarine and sugar until light and fluffy. Blend in the cocoa. Beat in the egg yolk and vanilla essence, then stir in the flour, baking powder and nutmeg. Blend in the cream until smooth. Cover and chill.

Roll out the dough to 5 mm/¼ in thick and cut out with a 5 cm/2 in cutter. Place the biscuits (cookies) on an ungreased baking (cookie) sheet and bake in a preheated oven at 200°C/400°F/gas mark 6 for 10 minutes until golden.

Chocolate-topped Biscuits

Makes 16

175 g/6 oz/¾ cup butter or margarine, softened

75 g/3 oz/1/3 cup caster (superfine) sugar

175 g/6 oz/1½ cups plain (all-purpose) flour

50 g/2 oz/½ cup ground rice

75 g/3 oz/¾ cup chocolate chips

100 g/4 oz/1 cup plain (semi-sweet) chocolate

Cream together the butter or margarine and sugar until light and fluffy. Mix in the flour and ground rice, then knead in the chocolate chips. Press into a greased Swiss roll tin (jelly roll pan) and prick with a fork. Bake in a preheated oven at 160°C/325°F/gas mark 3 for 30 minutes until golden. Mark into fingers while still warm, then leave to cool completely.

Melt the chocolate in a heatproof bowl over a pan of gently simmering water. Spread over the biscuits (cookies) and leave to cool and set before cutting into fingers. Store in an airtight container.

Coffee and Chocolate Sandwich Biscuits

Makes 40

For the biscuits (cookies):

175 g/6 oz/¾ cup butter or margarine

25 g/1 oz/2 tbsp lard (shortening)

450 g/1 lb/4 cups plain (all-purpose) flour

A pinch of salt

100 g/4 oz/½ cup soft brown sugar

5 ml/1 tsp bicarbonate of soda (baking soda)

60 ml/4 tbsp strong black coffee

5 ml/1 tsp vanilla essence (extract)

100 g/4 oz/1/3 cup golden (light corn) syrup

For the filling:

10 ml/2 tsp instant coffee powder

10 ml/2 tsp boiling water

50 g/2 oz/¼ cup caster (superfine) sugar

25 g/1 oz/2 tbsp butter or margarine

15 ml/1 tbsp milk

To make the biscuits, rub the butter or margarine and lard into the flour and salt until the mixture resembles bread-crumbs, then stir in the brown sugar. Mix the bicarbonate of soda with a little of the coffee, then stir into the mixture with the remaining coffee, the vanilla essence and the syrup and blend until you have a smooth dough. Place in a lightly oiled bowl, cover with clingfilm (plastic wrap) and leave overnight.

Roll out the dough on a lightly floured surface to about 1 cm/½ in thick and cut into 2 x 7.5 cm/¾ x 3 in rectangles. Score each one with a fork to make a ridged pattern. Transfer to a greased baking (cookie) sheet and bake in a preheated oven at 200°C/400°F/gas mark 6 for 10 minutes until golden brown. Cool on a wire rack.

To make the filling, dissolve the coffee powder in the boiling water in a small pan, then stir in the remaining ingredients and bring to the boil. Boil for 2 minutes, then remove from the heat and beat until thick and cool. Sandwich pairs of biscuits together with the filling.

Christmas Biscuits

Makes 24

100 g/4 oz/½ cup butter or margarine, softened

100 g/4 oz/½ cup caster (superfine) sugar

225 g/8 oz/2 cups plain (all-purpose) flour

A pinch of salt

5 ml/1 tsp ground cinnamon

1 egg yolk

10 ml/2 tsp cold water

A few drops of vanilla essence (extract)

For the icing (frosting):

225 g/8 oz/11/3 cups icing (confectioners') sugar, sifted

30 ml/2 tbsp water

Food colouring (optional)

Cream together the butter and sugar until light and fluffy. Fold in the flour, salt and cinnamon, then mix in the egg yolk, water and vanilla essence and mix to a firm dough. Wrap in clingfim (plastic wrap) and chill for 30 minutes.

Roll out the dough to 5 mm/¼ in thick and cut out Christmas shapes with biscuit (cookie) cutters or a sharp knife. Pierce a hole at the top of each biscuit if you want to hang them from a tree. Place the shapes on a greased baking (cookie) sheet and bake in a preheated oven at 200°C/ 400°F/gas mark 6 for 10 minutes until golden. Leave to cool.

To make the icing, gradually mix the water into the icing sugar until you have a fairly thick icing. Colour small quantities in different colours, if liked. Pipe patterns on to the biscuits, then leave to set. Thread a loop of ribbon or thread through the hole to hang up.

Coconut Biscuits

Makes 32

50 g/2 oz/3 tbsp golden (light corn) syrup

150 g/5 oz/2/3 cup butter or margarine

100 g/4 oz/½ cup caster (superfine) sugar

100 g/4 oz/1 cup plain (all-purpose) flour

75 g/3 oz/¾ cup rolled oats

50 g/2 oz/½ cup desiccated (shredded) coconut

10 ml/2 tsp bicarbonate of soda (baking soda)

15 ml/1 tbsp hot water

Melt together the syrup, butter or margarine and sugar. Stir in the flour, oats and desiccated coconut. Mix the bicarbonate of soda with the hot water, then stir into the other ingredients. Leave the mixture to cool slightly, then divide into 32 pieces and roll each one into a ball. Flatten the biscuits (cookies) and arrange on greased baking (cookie) sheets. Bake in a preheated oven at 160°C/325°F/gas mark 3 for 20 minutes until golden.

Corn Biscuits with Fruit Cream

Makes 12

150 g/5 oz/1¼ cups wholemeal (wholewheat) flour

150 g/5 oz/1¼ cups cornmeal

10 ml/2 tsp baking powder

A pinch of salt

225 g/8 oz/1 cup plain yoghurt

75 g/3 oz/¼ cup clear honey

2 eggs

45 ml/3 tbsp oil

For the fruit cream:
150 g/5 oz/2/3 cup butter or margarine, softened

Juice of 1 lemon

A few drops of vanilla essence (extract)

30 ml/2 tbsp caster (superfine) sugar

225 g/8 oz strawberries

Mix together the flour, cornmeal, baking powder and salt. Stir in the yoghurt, honey, eggs and oil and mix to a smooth dough. Roll out on a lightly floured surface to about 1 cm/½ in thick and cut into large rounds. Place on a greased baking (cookie) sheet and bake in a preheated oven at 200°C/400°F/gas mark 6 for 15 minutes until golden.

To make the fruit cream, blend together the butter or margarine, lemon juice, vanilla essence and sugar. Reserve a few strawberries for decoration, then purée the remainder and rub through a sieve (strainer) if you prefer the cream without seeds (pits). Mix into the butter mixture, then chill. Spoon or pipe a rosette of cream on to each biscuit before serving.

Cornish Biscuits

Makes 20

225 g/8 oz/2 cups self-raising (self-rising) flour

A pinch of salt

100 g/4 oz/½ cup butter or margarine

175 g/6 oz/2/3 cup caster (superfine) sugar

1 egg

Icing (confectioners') sugar, sifted, for dusting

Mix the flour and salt in a bowl, then rub in the butter or margarine until the mixture resembles breadcrumbs. Stir in the sugar. Stir in the egg and knead to a soft dough. Roll out thinly on a lightly floured surface, then cut into rounds.

Place on a greased baking (cookie) sheet and bake in a preheated oven at 200°C/400°F/gas mark 6 for about 10 minutes until golden.

Wholemeal Currant Biscuits

Makes 36

100 g/4 oz/½ cup butter or margarine, softened

50 g/2 oz/¼ cup demerara sugar

2 eggs, separated

100 g/4 oz/2/3 cup currants

225 g/8 oz/2 cups wholemeal (wholewheat) flour

100 g/4 oz/1 cup plain (all-purpose) flour

5 ml/1 tsp ground mixed (apple-pie) spice

150 ml/¼ pt/2/3 cup milk, plus extra for brushing

Cream together the butter or margarine and sugar together until light and fluffy. Beat in the egg yolks, then stir in the currants. Mix together the flours and mixed spice and stir into the mixture with the milk. Whisk the egg whites until they form soft peaks, then fold them into the mixture to make a soft dough. Roll out the dough on a lightly floured surface, then cut out with a 5 cm/2 in biscuit (cookie) cutter. Place on a greased baking (cookie) sheet and brush with milk. Bake in a preheated oven at 180°C/350°F/gas mark 4 for 20 minutes until golden.

Date Sandwich Biscuits

Makes 30

225 g/8 oz/1 cup butter or margarine, softened

450 g/1 lb/2 cups soft brown sugar

225 g/8 oz/2 cups oatmeal

225 g/8 oz/2 cups plain (all-purpose) flour

2.5 ml/½ tsp bicarbonate of soda (baking soda)

A pinch of salt

120 ml/4 fl oz/½ cup milk

225 g/8 oz/2 cups stoned (pitted) dates, very finely chopped

250 ml/8 fl oz/1 cup water

Cream together the butter or margarine and half the sugar until light and fluffy. Mix together the dry ingredients and add to the creamed mixture alternately with the milk until you have a firm dough. Roll out on a lightly floured board and cut into rounds with a biscuit (cookie) cutter. Place on a greased baking (cookie) sheet and bake in a preheated oven at 180°C/350°F/gas mark 4 for 10 minutes until golden.

Place all the remaining ingredients in a pan and bring to the boil. Reduce the heat and simmer for 20 minutes until thickened, stirring occasionally. Leave to cool. Sandwich the biscuits together with the filling.

Digestive Biscuits (Graham Crackers)

Makes 24

175 g/6 oz/1½ cups wholemeal (wholewheat) flour

50 g/2 oz/½ cup plain (all-purpose) flour

50 g/2 oz/½ cup medium oatmeal

2.5 ml/½ tsp salt

5 ml/1 tsp baking powder

100 g/4 oz/½ cup butter or margarine

30 ml/2 tbsp soft brown sugar

60 ml/4 tbsp milk

Mix together the flours, oatmeal, salt and baking powder, then rub in the butter or margarine and mix in the sugar. Gradually add the milk and mix to a soft dough. Knead well until no longer sticky. Roll out to 5 mm/¼ in thick and cut into 5 cm/2 in rounds with a biscuit (cookie) cutter. Place on a greased baking (cookie) sheet and bake in a preheated oven at 180°C/350°F/gas mark 4 for about 15 minutes.

Easter Biscuits

Makes 20

75 g/3 oz/1/3 cup butter or margarine, softened

100 g/4 oz/½ cup caster (superfine) sugar

1 egg yolk

150 g/6 oz/1½ cups self-raising (self-rising) flour

5 ml/1 tsp ground mixed (apple-pie) spice

15 ml/1 tbsp chopped mixed (candied) peel

50 g/2 oz/1/3 cup currants

15 ml/1 tbsp milk

Caster (superfine) sugar for sprinkling

Cream together the butter or margarine and sugar. Beat in the egg yolk, then fold in the flour and mixed spice. Stir in the peel and currants with enough of the milk to make a stiff dough. Roll out to about 5 mm/¼ in thick and cut into 5 cm/2 in rounds with a biscuit (cookie) cutter. Place the biscuits on a greased baking (cookie) sheet and prick with a fork. Bake in a preheated oven at 180°C/350°F/gas mark 4 for about 20 minutes until golden. Sprinkle with sugar.

Florentines

Makes 40

100 g/4 oz/½ cup butter or margarine

100 g/4 oz/½ cup caster (superfine) sugar

15 ml/1 tbsp double (heavy) cream

100 g/4 oz/1 cup chopped mixed nuts

75 g/3 oz/½ cup sultanas (golden raisins)

50 g/2 oz/¼ cup glacé (candied) cherries

Melt the butter or margarine, sugar and cream in a pan over a low heat. Remove from the heat and stir in the nuts, sultanas and glacé cherries. Drop teaspoonfuls, well apart, on to greased baking (cookie) sheets lined with rice paper. Bake in a preheated oven at 180°C/ 350°F/gas mark 4 for 10 minutes. Leave to cool on the sheets for 5 minutes, then transfer to a wire rack to finish cooling, trimming off the excess rice paper.

Chocolate Florentines

Makes 40

100 g/4 oz/½ cup butter or margarine

100 g/4 oz/½ cup caster (superfine) sugar

15 ml/1 tbsp double (heavy) cream

100 g/4 oz/1 cup chopped mixed nuts

75 g/3 oz/½ cup sultanas (golden raisins)

50 g/2 oz/¼ cup glacé (candied) cherries

100 g/4 oz/1 cup plain (semi-sweet) chocolate

Melt the butter or margarine, sugar and cream in a pan over a low heat. Remove from the heat and stir in the nuts, sultanas and glacé cherries. Drop teaspoonfuls, well apart, on to greased baking (cookie) sheets lined with rice paper. Bake in a preheated oven at 180°C/ 350°F/gas mark 4 for 10 minutes. Leave to cool on the sheets for 5 minutes, then transfer to a wire rack to finish cooling, trimming off the excess rice paper.

Melt the chocolate in a heatproof bowl set over a pan of gently simmering water. Spread over the top of the biscuits (cookies) and leave to cool and set.

Luxury Chocolate Florentines

Makes 40

100 g/4 oz/½ cup butter or margarine

100 g/4 oz/½ cup soft brown sugar

15 ml/1 tbsp double (heavy) cream

50 g/2 oz/¼ cup almonds, chopped

50 g/2 oz/¼ cup hazelnuts, chopped

75 g/3 oz/½ cup sultanas (golden raisins)

50 g/2 oz/¼ cup glacé (candied) cherries

100 g/4 oz/1 cup plain (semi-sweet) chocolate

50 g/2 oz/½ cup white chocolate

Melt the butter or margarine, sugar and cream in a pan over a low heat. Remove from the heat and stir in the nuts, sultanas and glacé cherries. Drop teaspoonfuls, well apart, on to greased baking (cookie) sheets lined with rice paper. Bake in a preheated oven at 180°C/ 350°F/gas mark 4 for 10 minutes. Leave to cool on the sheets for 5 minutes, then transfer to a wire rack to finish cooling, trimming off the excess rice paper.

Melt the plain chocolate in a heatproof bowl set over a pan of gently simmering water. Spread over the top of the biscuits (cookies) and leave to cool and set. Melt the white chocolate in a clean bowl in the same way, then drizzle lines of white chocolate across the biscuits in a random pattern.

Fudge Nut Biscuits

Makes 30

75 g/3 oz/1/3 cup butter or margarine, softened

200 g/7 oz/scant 1 cup caster (superfine) sugar

1 egg, lightly beaten

100 g/4 oz/½ cup cottage cheese

5 ml/1 tsp vanilla essence (extract)

150 g/5 oz/1¼ cups plain (all-purpose) flour

25 g/1 oz/¼ cup cocoa (unsweetened chocolate) powder

2.5 ml/½ tsp baking powder

1.5 ml/¼ tsp bicarbonate of soda (baking soda)

A pinch of salt

25 g/1 oz/¼ cup chopped mixed nuts

25 g/1 oz/2 tbsp granulated sugar

Cream together the butter or margarine and caster sugar until light and fluffy. Gradually mix in the egg and cottage cheese. Stir in the remaining ingredients except the granulated sugar and mix to a soft dough. Wrap in clingfilm (plastic wrap) and chill for 1 hour.

Roll the dough into walnut-sized balls and roll in the granulated sugar. Place the biscuits (cookies) on a greased baking (cookie) sheet and bake in a preheated oven at 180°C/350°F/gas mark 4 for 10 minutes.

German Iced Biscuits

Makes 12

50 g/2 oz/¼ cup butter or margarine

100 g/4 oz/1 cup plain (all-purpose) flour

25 g/1 oz/2 tbsp caster (superfine) sugar

60 ml/4 tbsp blackberry jam (conserve)

100 g/4 oz/2/3 cup icing (confectioners') sugar, sifted

15 ml/1 tbsp lemon juice

Rub the butter into the flour until the mixture resembles breadcrumbs. Stir in the sugar and press to a paste. Roll out to 5 mm/¼ in thick and cut into rounds with a biscuit (cookie) cutter. Place on a greased baking (cookie) sheet and bake in a preheated oven at 180°C/350°F/gas mark 6 for 10 minutes until cold. Leave to cool.

Sandwich pairs of biscuits together with the jam. Place the icing sugar in a bowl and make a well in the centre. Gradually mix in the lemon juice to make a glacé icing (frosting). Drizzle over the biscuits, then leave to set.

Gingersnaps

Makes 24

300 g/10 oz/1¼ cups butter or margarine, softened

225 g/8 oz/1 cup soft brown sugar

75 g/3 oz/¼ cup black treacle (molasses)

1 egg

250 g/9 oz/2¼ cups plain (all-purpose) flour

10 ml/2 tsp bicarbonate of soda (baking soda)

2.5 ml/½ tsp salt

5 ml/1 tsp ground ginger

5 ml/1 tsp ground cloves

5 ml/1 tsp ground cinnamon

50 g/2 oz/¼ cup granulated sugar

Cream together the butter or margarine, brown sugar, treacle and egg together until fluffy. Mix together the flour, bicarbonate of soda, salt and spices. Stir into the butter mixture and mix to a firm dough. Cover and chill for 1 hour.

Shape the dough into small balls and roll in the granulated sugar. Place well apart on a greased baking (cookie) sheet and sprinkle with a little water. Bake in a preheated oven at 190°C/375°F/gas 5 for 12 minutes until golden and crisp.

Ginger Biscuits

Makes 24

100 g/4 oz/½ cup butter or margarine

225 g/8 oz/2 cups self-raising (self-rising) flour

5 ml/1 tsp bicarbonate of soda (baking soda)

5 ml/1 tsp ground ginger

100 g/4 oz/½ cup caster (superfine) sugar

45 ml/3 tbsp golden (light corn) syrup, warmed

Rub the butter or margarine into the flour, bicarbonate of soda and ginger. Stir in the sugar, then blend in the syrup and mix to a stiff dough. Roll into walnut-sized balls, place well apart on a greased baking (cookie) sheet and press down lightly with a fork to flatten. Bake the biscuits (cookies) in a preheated oven at 190°C/375°F/gas mark 5 for 10 minutes.

Gingerbread Men

Makes about 16

350 g/12 oz/3 cups self-raising (self-rising) flour

A pinch of salt

10 ml/2 tsp ground ginger

100 g/4 oz/1/3 cup golden (light corn) syrup

75 g/3 oz/1/3 cup butter or margarine

25 g/1 oz/2 tbsp caster (superfine) sugar

1 egg, lightly beaten

A few currants (optional)

Mix together the flour, salt and ginger. Melt the syrup, butter or margarine and sugar in a pan. Leave to cool slightly, then beat into the dry ingredients with the egg and mix to a firm dough. Roll out on a lightly floured surface to 5 mm/¼ in thick and cut out with shaped cutters. The number you can make will depend on the size of your cutters. Place on a lightly greased baking (cookie) sheet and gently press currants into the biscuits (cookies) for eyes and buttons, if liked. Bake in a preheated oven at 180°C/350°F/gas mark 4 for 15 minutes until golden brown and firm to the touch.

Wholemeal Ginger Biscuits

Makes 24

200 g/7 oz/1¾ cups wholemeal (wholewheat) flour

10 ml/2 tsp baking powder

10 ml/2 tsp ground ginger

100 g/4 oz/½ cup butter or margarine

50 g/2 oz/¼ cup soft brown sugar

60 ml/4 tbsp clear honey

Mix together the flour, baking powder and ginger. Melt the butter or margarine with the sugar and honey, then stir it into the dry ingredients and mix to a firm dough. Roll out on a floured surface and cut into rounds with a biscuit (cookie) cutter. Place on a greased baking (cookie) sheet and bake in a preheated oven at 190°C/375°F/gas mark 5 for 12 minutes until golden and crisp.

Ginger and Rice Biscuits

Makes 12

225 g/8 oz/2 cups plain (all-purpose) flour

2.5 ml/½ tsp ground mace

10 ml/2 tsp ground ginger

75 g/3 oz/1/3 cup butter or margarine

175 g/6 oz/¾ cup caster (superfine) sugar

1 egg, beaten

5 ml/1 tsp lemon juice

30 ml/2 tbsp ground rice

Mix together the flour and spices, rub in the butter or margarine until the mixture resembles breadcrumbs, then stir in the sugar. Mix in the egg and lemon juice to a firm dough and knead gently until smooth. Dust a work surface with the ground rice and roll out the dough to 1 cm/½ in thick. Cut into 5 cm/2 in rounds with a biscuit (cookie) cutter. Arrange on a greased baking (cookie) sheet and bake in a preheated oven at 180°C/350°F/gas mark 4 for 20 minutes until firm to the touch.

Golden Biscuits

Makes 36

75 g/3 oz/1/3 cup butter or margarine, softened

200 g/7 oz/scant 1 cup caster (superfine) sugar

2 eggs, lightly beaten

225 g/8 oz/2 cups plain (all-purpose) flour

10 ml/2 tsp baking powder

5 ml/1 tsp grated nutmeg

A pinch of salt

Egg or milk for glazing

Caster (superfine) sugar for sprinkling

Cream together the butter or margarine and sugar. Gradually mix in the eggs, then stir in the flour, baking powder, nutmeg and salt and mix to a soft dough. Cover and leave to rest for 30 minutes.

Roll out the dough on a lightly floured surface to about 5 mm/¼ in thick and cut into rounds with a biscuit (cookie) cutter. Place on a greased baking (cookie) sheet, brush with beaten egg or milk and sprinkle with sugar. Bake in a preheated oven at 200°C/400°F/gas mark 6 for 8–10 minutes until golden.

Hazelnut Biscuits

Makes 24

100 g/4 oz/½ cup butter or margarine, softened

50 g/2 oz/¼ cup caster (superfine) sugar

100 g/4 oz/1 cup plain (all-purpose) flour

25 g/1 oz/¼ cup ground hazelnuts

Cream together the butter or margarine and sugar until light and fluffy. Gradually work in the flour and nuts until you have a stiff dough. Roll into small balls and place, well apart, on a greased baking (cookie) sheet. Bake the biscuits (cookies) in a preheated oven at 180°C/ 350°F/gas mark 4 for 20 minutes.

Crunchy Hazelnut Biscuits

Makes 40

100 g/4 oz/½ cup butter or margarine, softened

100 g/4 oz/½ cup caster (superfine) sugar

1 egg, beaten

5 ml/1 tsp vanilla essence (extract)

175 g/6 oz/1½ cups plain (all-purpose) flour

50 g/2 oz/½ cup ground hazelnuts

50 g/2 oz/½ cup hazelnuts, chopped

Cream together the butter or margarine and sugar until light and fluffy. Gradually beat in the egg and vanilla essence, then fold in the flour, ground hazelnuts and hazelnuts and knead to a dough. Roll into a ball, wrap in clingfim (plastic wrap) and chill for 1 hour.

Roll out the dough to 5 mm/¼ in thick and cut into rounds with a biscuit (cookie) cutter. Arrange on a greased baking (cookie) sheet and bake in a preheated oven at 200°C/400°F/gas mark 6 for 10 minutes until golden.

Hazelnut and Almond Biscuits

Makes 24

100 g/4 oz/½ cup butter or margarine, softened

75 g/3 oz/½ cup icing (confectioners') sugar, sifted

50 g/2 oz/1/3 cup ground hazelnuts

50 g/2 oz/1/3 cup ground almonds

100 g/4 oz/1 cup plain (all-purpose) flour

5 ml/1 tsp almond essence (extract)

A pinch of salt

Cream the butter or margarine and sugar until light and fluffy. Mix in the remaining ingredients to make a stiff dough. Roll into a ball, cover with clingfilm (plastic wrap) and chill for 30 minutes.

Roll out the dough to about 1 cm/ ½ in thick and cut into rounds with a biscuit (cookie) cutter. Place on a greased baking (cookie) sheet and bake in a preheated oven at 180°C/350°F/gas mark 4 for 15 minutes until golden brown.

Honey Cookies

Makes 24

75 g/3 oz/1/3 cup butter or margarine

100 g/4 oz/1/3 cup set honey

225 g/8 oz/2 cups wholemeal (wholewheat) flour

5 ml/1 tsp baking powder

A pinch of salt

50 g/2 oz/¼ cup muscovado sugar

5 ml/1 tsp ground cinnamon

1 egg, lightly beaten

Melt the butter or margarine and honey until blended. Stir in the remaining ingredients. Place spoonfuls of the mixture well apart on a greased baking (cookie) sheet and bake in a preheated oven at 180°C/350°F/gas mark 4 for 15 minutes until golden. Leave to cool for 5 minutes before transferring to a wire rack to finish cooling.

Honey Ratafias

Makes 24

2 egg whites

100 g/4 oz/1 cup ground almonds

A few drops of almond essence (extract)

100 g/4 oz/1/3 cup clear honey

Rice paper

Beat the egg whites until stiff. Carefully fold in the almonds, almond essence and honey. Place spoonfuls of the mixture well apart on baking (cookie) sheets lined with rice paper and bake in a preheated oven at 180°C/350°F/gas mark 4 for 15 minutes until golden. Leave to cool slightly, then tear round the paper to remove.

Honey and Buttermilk Biscuits

Makes 12

50 g/2 oz/¼ cup butter or margarine

225 g/8 oz/2 cups self-raising (self-rising) flour

175 ml/6 fl oz/¾ cup buttermilk

45 ml/3 tbsp clear honey

Rub the butter or margarine into the flour until the mixture resembles breadcrumbs. Stir in the buttermilk and honey and mix to a stiff dough. Place on a lightly floured surface and knead until smooth, then roll out to 2 cm/¾ in thick and cut into 5 cm/2 in round with a biscuit (cookie) cutter. Place on a greased baking (cookie) sheet and bake in a preheated oven at 230°C/450°F/gas mark 8 for 10 minutes until golden brown.

Lemon Butter Biscuits

Makes 20

100 g/4 oz/1 cup ground rice

100 g/4 oz/1 cup plain (all-purpose) flour

75 g/3 oz/1/3 cup caster (superfine) sugar

A pinch of salt

2.5 ml/½ tsp baking powder

100 g/4 oz/½ cup butter or margarine

Grated rind of 1 lemon

1 egg, beaten

Mix together the ground rice, flour, sugar, salt and baking powder. Rub in the butter until the mixture resembles breadcrumbs. Stir in the lemon rind and mix with enough of the egg to form a firm dough. Knead gently, then roll out on a floured surface and cut into shapes with a biscuit (cookie) cutter. Place on a greased baking (cookie) sheet and bake in a preheated oven at 180°C/350°F/gas mark 4 for 30 minutes. Leave to cool slightly on the sheet, then transfer to a wire rack to cool completely.

Lemon Cookies

Makes 24

100 g/4 oz/½ cup butter or margarine

100 g/4 oz/½ cup caster (superfine) sugar

1 egg, lightly beaten

225 g/8 oz/2 cups plain (all-purpose) flour

5 ml/1 tsp baking powder

Grated rind of ½ lemon

5 ml/1 tsp lemon juice

30 ml/2 tbsp demerara sugar

Melt the butter or margarine and caster sugar over a low heat, stirring continuously, until the mixture begins to thicken. Remove from the heat and stir in the egg, flour, baking powder, lemon rind and juice and mix to a dough. Cover and chill for 30 minutes.

Shape the dough into small balls and arrange on a greased baking (cookie) sheet, pressing flat with a fork. Sprinkle with the demerara sugar. Bake in a preheated oven at 180°C/350°F/gas mark 4 for 15 minutes.

Melting Moments

Makes 16

100 g/4 oz/½ cup butter or margarine, softened

75 g/3 oz/1/3 cup caster (superfine) sugar

1 egg, beaten

150 g/5 oz/1¼ cups plain (all-purpose) flour

10 ml/2 tsp baking powder

A pinch of salt

8 glacé (candied) cherries, halved

Cream together the butter or margarine and sugar until light and fluffy. Gradually beat in the egg, then fold in the flour, baking powder and salt. Knead gently to a smooth dough. Shape the dough into 16 equal-sized balls and place, well apart, on a greased baking (cookie) sheet. Flatten slightly, then top each one with a cherry half. Bake in a preheated oven at 180°C/350°F/gas mark 4 for 15 minutes. Leave to cool on the sheet for 5 minutes, then transfer to a wire rack to finish cooling.